Maths Progress

International 11–14

Confidence • Fluency • Problem-solving • Progression

9

Workbook

Pearson

Published by Pearson Education Limited, 80 Strand, London, WC2R 0RL.

www.pearsonschoolsandfecolleges.co.uk

Text © Pearson Education Limited 2020
Project managed and edited by Just Content Ltd
Typeset by PDQ Digital Media Solutions Ltd
Original illustrations © Pearson Education Limited 2020
Cover illustration by Robert Samuel Hanson

The rights of Greg Byrd, Keith Gallick, Catherine Murphy, Su Nicholson and Diane Oliver to be identified as authors of this work have been asserted by them in accordance with the Copyright, Designs and Patents Act 1988.

First published 2020

24

10 9 8 7

British Library Cataloguing in Publication Data
A catalogue record for this book is available from the British Library.

ISBN 978 1 292 32720 4

Printed in Great Britain by Bell and Bain Ltd, Glasgow

Acknowledgements
The publisher would like to thank Diane Oliver for her input and advice.

Note from the publisher
Pearson has robust editorial processes, including answer and fact checks, to ensure the accuracy of the content in this publication, and every effort is made to ensure this publication is free of errors. We are, however, only human, and occasionally errors do occur. Pearson is not liable for any misunderstandings that arise as a result of errors in this publication, but it is our priority to ensure that the content is accurate. If you spot an error, please do contact us at resourcescorrections@pearson.com so we can make sure it is corrected.

Contents

Welcome to Maths Progress International Workbooks

Starting a new course is exciting! We believe you will have fun with maths, while at the same time nurturing your confidence and raising your achievement. Here's how:

Start by **Mastering** fundamental knowledge and skills over a series of lessons.

Guided questions and partially worked solutions help you structure your answers.

Your teacher has online access to **Answers**.

A **confidence checker** at the end of every lesson helps you keep track of your strengths and weaknesses and suggests which questions from **Strengthen** you should try.

QR codes give you direct access to worked example videos via your phone or tablet, providing plenty of support for tricky questions.

As well as hints that help you with specific questions, you'll find **Literacy hints** (to explain some unfamiliar terms) and **Strategy hints** (to help with working out).

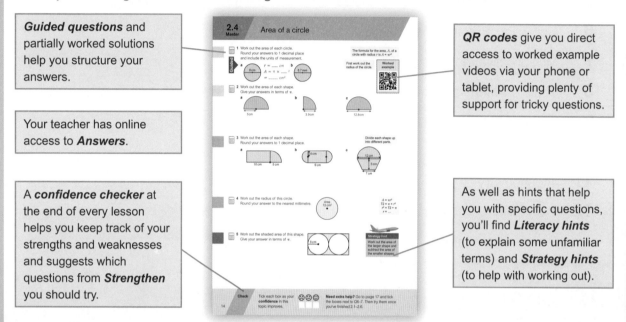

Choose only the topics in **Strengthen** that you need a bit more practice with. You'll find more hints here to lead you through specific questions.

Extend helps you to apply the maths you know to some different situations.

When you have finished the whole unit, a **Unit test** helps you see how much progress you are making. Keep track of your confidence and the questions you answered correctly in the Progression charts on pages 124–127.

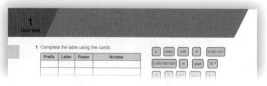

Guided

1 Complete the place-value table showing the powers of 10.

$\div 10 \quad \div 10 \quad \div 10 \quad \div 10 \quad \div 10 \quad \div 10 \quad \div 10 \quad \div 10$

....	100	10	1	.	$\frac{1}{10}$	$\frac{1}{100}$	$\frac{1}{1000}$	$\frac{1}{10000}$	....
....	$10^{...}$	$10^{...}$	10^0	.	10^{-1}	$10^{...}$	$10^{...}$	$10^{...}$	....

$\div 10 \quad \div 10 \quad \div 10 \quad \div 10 \quad \div 10 \quad \div 10 \quad \div 10 \quad \div 10$

Each of the headings in the place-value table is a power of 10. This is because we have a decimal system (*dec* = 10).

2 a The tables show the prefixes for powers of 10. Complete the tables.

Prefix	Letter	Power	Number
tera	T		1 000 000 000 000
giga	G	10^9	1 000 000 000
mega	M		1 000 000
kilo	k	10^3	
deci	d	10^{-1}	0.1

Prefix	Letter	Power	Number
centi	c	10^{-2}	
milli	m		0.001
micro	μ	10^{-6}	
nano	n		0.000 000 001
pico	p	10^{-12}	

b How many times bigger is

i a gigawatt than a megawatt ....

ii a megametre than a metre ....

iii a kilometre than a decimetre ....

iv a centimetre than a nanometre? ....

Some powers of 10 have a name called a prefix.
Each prefix is represented by a letter.
The prefix for 10^6 is mega (M) as in megabyte (MB).

Literacy hint

The prefix for micro is the Greek letter μ, pronounced 'mu'.

3 STEM The table shows information about three of the planets.

Guided

Name of planet	Diameter of planet (km)	Average distance from Sun (km)
Earth	$1.28 \times 10^4 = 12\ 800$	$1.5 \times 10^8 =$ ....
Mars	$6.8 \times 10^3 =$	$2.28 \times 10^8 =$ ....
Jupiter	$1.43 \times 10^5 =$	$7.79 \times 10^8 =$ ....

a Complete the table, writing the distances as ordinary numbers.

b Which of these planets has the greatest diameter? ....

c Which of these planets is closest to the Sun? ....

First write 10^4 as an ordinary number.
$1.28 \times 10^4 =$
$1.28 \times 10\ 000 = \square$

4 STEM / Problem-solving A jumbo jet has a maximum take-off mass of 3.3×10^5 kg. How many tonnes is this?

1 tonne = 1000 kg

5 STEM / Reasoning Mycoplasma are the smallest living cells yet discovered. They can be as small as 1.5 micrometres in diameter. What is this diameter in millimetres?

Check Tick each box as your **confidence** in this topic improves. **Need extra help?** Go to page 6 and tick the box next to Q1. Then try it once you've finished 1.1–1.5.

1

Guided

1 Evaluate (work out the value of) these.

You can simplify expressions containing powers to make calculations easier.

a $\dfrac{2 \times 5^6}{5^4} = 2 \times 5^{\cdots} = 2 \times \text{.......} = \text{.......}$

Simplify the powers of 5, then multiply by 2.

b $\dfrac{2^3 \times 4^9}{4^8}$ ....

c $\dfrac{5 \times 3^7}{3^3 \times 3^2}$ ....

2 Problem-solving Work out $\dfrac{8 \times 2^{10} \times 5 \times 32}{2^6 \times 16 \times 2^7}$

Strategy hint

Write as many numbers as possible as powers of 2.

3 Sort these cards into matching pairs.

| $19 + 3^2$ | $19 - 3^2$ | $19 + (-3)^2$ | $19 - (-3)^2$ |

| $34 - 5^2 - 4^2$ | $34 - (-5)^2 + 4^2$ | $34 - 5^2 + (-4)^2$ | $34 - (-5)^2 - 4^2$ |

4 Round these numbers to the given number of significant figures.

Guided

a 52.5381 (4 s.f.)

52.54

When the next digit is 5 or above, round the previous digit up. Here the fifth significant figure is an 8, so round the 3 up to 4.

You can round numbers to a given number of significant figures (s.f.). The first significant figure is the one with the highest place value. It is the first non-zero digit in the number, counting from the left.

b 0.004 721 (3 s.f.)

The fourth significant figure is 1, so leave the third digit as 2.

c 85 739 (2 s.f.)

The third significant figure is 7.

5 Estimate the answer to each calculation by rounding each number to 1 significant figure.

a 54 × 279 ....   **b** 4268 × 37 ....   **c** 487 ÷ 18 ....

50 × 300 = ☐

6 Estimate the answer to each calculation by rounding each number to 1 significant figure.

a $\dfrac{(3.4 + 5.8)^2}{2.3^3}$

$\dfrac{(3.4 + 5.8)^2}{2.3^3} \approx \dfrac{(3 + 6)^2}{2^3} = \dfrac{9^2}{8}$

What number is a multiple of 8 and close to 9^2? Use this to estimate the final answer.

b $\dfrac{(34 - 17)^2}{6.7^2}$

c $\dfrac{5.2 \times 4.7}{(1.8 + 3.4)^2}$

7 Problem-solving Prem starts with a whole number.
He rounds it to 2 significant figures. His answer is 430.
Write down the largest and smallest numbers he could have started with.

8 Real The table shows the capacities of five football stadiums.

Stadium	Old Trafford	Anfield	Deva	Emirates	Cardiff City
Capacity	75 731	45 522	5376	60 362	26 828

a In the last row in the table, round each capacity correct to 1 s.f.

b Work out an estimate of the range in capacities.

Check Tick each box as your **confidence** in this topic improves.

Need extra help? Go to page 6 and tick the boxes next to Q2 and 3. Then try them once you've finished 1.1–1.5.

Guided

1 Complete

a $5^{-2} = \dfrac{1}{5^2}$ **b** $\dfrac{1}{2} = 2^{\cdots}$ **c** $7^{\cdots} = \dfrac{1}{49}$

d $\ldots^{-2} = \dfrac{1}{121}$ **e** $3^{-3} = \ldots$ **f** $2^{-5} = \ldots$

g $8^{-1} = \ldots$ **h** $\dfrac{1}{16} = 4^{\cdots} = 2^{\cdots}$ **i** $\dfrac{1}{625} = 25^{\cdots} = 5^{\cdots}$

> A number raised to a negative power is the same as the reciprocal of that number to the power.

2 Write each calculation as a single power.

a $10^7 \times 10^{-4}$ **b** $6^3 \times 6^{-5}$ **c** $3^{-2} \times 3^{-4}$

    $= 10^3$ —— $\boxed{10^7 \times 10^{-4} = 10^{7+(-4)}}$

d $5^{-2} \div 5^3$ **e** $9^{-8} \div 9^{-3}$ **f** $(11^{-3})^4$ **g** $(4^{-6})^2$

> The laws of indices still apply with negative numbers.
> $a^m \times a^n = a^{m+n}$
> $a^m \div a^n = a^{m-n}$
> $(a^m)^n = a^{mn}$

3 Write each calculation as

   i a single power

   ii an integer or a fraction.

a $6^5 \times 6^{-3} \times 6^{-4}$ **b** $3^{-5} \times 3^{-1} \div 3^{-9}$ **c** $\dfrac{5^{-4} \times 5^{-7}}{5^{-8}}$

   i ....   **i** ....   **i** ....

   ii ....   **ii** ....   **ii** ....

> **Worked example**
>

4 Write each calculation as a fraction.

a $\dfrac{1}{5} \times \dfrac{1}{5}$ **b** $\left(\dfrac{5}{8}\right)^2$ **c** $\left(\dfrac{3}{10}\right)^3$

> The brackets show that the whole fraction (the numerator and denominator) is squared or cubed.

5 Write each number as a fraction raised to a power.

a $\dfrac{25}{49}$ **b** $\dfrac{64}{144}$ **c** $\dfrac{81}{100}$

d $\dfrac{9}{121}$ **e** $\dfrac{8}{27}$ **f** $\dfrac{1}{125}$

6 Problem-solving Jai eats half a pizza, his dad eats half of what is left and his mum eats half of what is then left. How much pizza remains? Write your answer

a as a fraction

b as a fraction raised to a power.

Check   Tick each box as your **confidence** in this topic improves.   ☹ 😐 ☺   **Need extra help?** Go to page 6 and tick the boxes next to Q4 and 5. Then try them once you've finished 1.1–1.5.

1 Circle the numbers that are written in standard form.

3.5×10^8 2×10^7 0.6×10^4

9.9×10 73×10^{-8} 4.306×10^{-9}

> A number written in **standard form** is a number between 1 and 10 multiplied by a power of 10.
> 4.2×10^6 is written in standard form.
> Using algebra, standard form is $A \times 10^n$ where $1 \leqslant A < 10$ and n is an integer.

2 These numbers are written in standard form.
Write them as ordinary numbers.

a 5×10^3 **b** 3.7×10^{-4} **c** 4.9×10^7 **d** 2.09×10^{-6} $5 \times 10^3 = 5 \times 1000 = \square$

3 Write each number in standard form.

Guided

a 35 700

    $= 3.57 \times 10^4$

> 3.57 lies between 1 and 10. Multiply by the power of 10 needed to give the original number
> 3 . 5   7   0   0

b 498

> 1.8 lies between 1 and 10. Multiply by the power of 10 needed to give the original number. The number is less than 1 so the power is negative. This is the same as dividing by a power of 10.
> 0 . 0   0   1   8

c 7 100 000

d 0.0018

    $= 1.8 \times 10^{-3}$

e 0.000 006 35

f 0.000 000 04

4 STEM

a Write each of the distances in the table in standard form.

Object	Average distance from Earth (km)	Average distance from Earth in standard form (km)
Mars	225 000 000	
Our Moon	384 400	
Saturn	1 300 000 000	

Worked example

b Jupiter is at an average distance of 7.87×10^8 km from Earth. Is it closer to Earth than Saturn?

5 Put each set of numbers in order, from smallest to largest.

a 6.4×10^3 7.8×10^2 2.1×10^4 8.52×10^2 3.51×10^4

> Write each number in full to help you order them.

b 1.4×10^{-4} 9.27×10^{-6} 5.31×10^{-5} 6.8×10^{-4} 2.67×10^{-3}

6 STEM Write these sub-atomic particles in order of their mass, largest first.

Particle	electron	neutron	proton
Mass (g)	9.11×10^{-28}	1.675×10^{-24}	1.673×10^{-24}

7 STEM Write the following measurements as ordinary numbers

    i in metres   **ii** in millimetres.

> There are 1000 mm in 1 m, so multiply by $10^\square$.

a The diameter of a human hair: 1×10^{-4} m   **i** ....   **ii** ....

b The width of a cheek cell nucleus: 5.1×10^{-6} m   **i** ....   **ii** ....

Check   Tick each box as your **confidence** in this topic improves.   **Need extra help?** Go to pages 6 and 7 and tick the boxes next to Q6–10. Then try them once you've finished 1.1–1.5.

Guided

1 Work out each calculation.
Give your answer in standard form.

> Rearrange so that the numbers are together and the powers of 10 are together.

a $(1.3 \times 10^4) \times (8 \times 10^5)$

$= 1.3 \times 8 \times 10^4 \times 10^5$

> Calculate the product of the numbers and use laws of indices to simplify the powers of 10.

$= 10.4 \times 10^9$

$= 1.04 \times 10 \times 10^9$

> Rewrite the answer in standard form, if necessary: $10.4 = 1.04 \times 10^1$

$= 1.04 \times 10^{10}$

b $(2.85 \times 10^6) \times (4 \times 10)$ **c** $(4.2 \times 10^3) \times (6 \times 10^7)$ **d** $(1.5 \times 10^4)^2$

2 Work out each calculation. Give your answers in standard form.

a $\dfrac{8 \times 10^6}{4 \times 10^2}$ **b** $\dfrac{9 \times 10^7}{3 \times 10^4}$ **c** $\dfrac{1.8 \times 10^5}{6 \times 10}$

> Divide the number parts. Use the laws of indices to divide the powers of 10.

3 Use a calculator to work out

a $(3.58 \times 10^2) \times (7.25 \times 10^5)$ **b** $\dfrac{1.457 \times 10^{12}}{3.1 \times 10^7}$

> **Worked example**
>

4 **STEM** An optical microscope magnifies objects 1000 times.
A red blood cell has a diameter of 1×10^{-5} m.
How large will it appear under the microscope?
Give your answer in millimetres.

5 Work out each calculation. Give your answers in standard form.

a $3.2 \times 10^5 + 2.47 \times 10^5$ **b** $4.5 \times 10^4 + 2.7 \times 10^3$

c $5.8 \times 10^{-6} - 1.4 \times 10^{-6}$ **d** $2.9 \times 10^{-5} - 6.5 \times 10^{-7}$

> Both numbers need to have the same power of 10 before you can add or subtract them. Alternatively, you can convert from standard form to ordinary numbers first.

6 **STEM** Viruses vary in size from the smallest at 1.7×10^{-9} m to the largest at 1×10^{-6} m.
What is the range in the sizes of viruses?

Check Tick each box as your **confidence** in this topic improves. ☹ 😐 ☺

Need extra help? Go to page 7 and tick the box next to Q11. Then try it once you've finished 1.1–1.5.

5

Powers of 10

1 Convert

   a 4.7 Gm to km ....

   b 0.000 53 mm to nm ....

   c 829 000 μm to km ....

   d 0.043 μm to pm ....

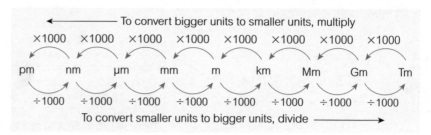

To convert bigger units to smaller units, multiply

×1000 ×1000 ×1000 ×1000 ×1000 ×1000 ×1000 ×1000

pm   nm   μm   mm   m   km   Mm   Gm   Tm

÷1000 ÷1000 ÷1000 ÷1000 ÷1000 ÷1000 ÷1000 ÷1000

To convert smaller units to bigger units, divide

Calculating and estimating

2 Round each number to 1 significant figure.

   a 47.23 ....

   > Circle the first significant figure. It's in the 10s column, so round to the nearest 10.

   c 55 500 ....

   b 0.73 ....

   d 0.0184 ....

3 Estimate the answer to each calculation by rounding each number to 1 significant figure.

   a 365×45 ....

   b $5631 \div 23$ ....

Indices

4 a i $4^3 \div 4^8 = 4^{\cdots}$

   ii $4^3 \div 4^8 = \dfrac{4^3}{4^8} = \dfrac{\cancel{4} \times \cancel{4} \times \cancel{4}}{\cancel{4} \times \cancel{4} \times \cancel{4} \times 4 \times 4 \times 4 \times 4 \times 4} = \dfrac{\cdots}{\cdots}$

   > Which index rule can you use?

   iii Use your answers to complete: $4^{-5} = \dfrac{1}{4^{\cdots}}$

> Worked example

   b Complete

   i $5^{-2} = \dfrac{1}{5^{\cdots}}$ **ii** $3^{-4} = \dfrac{1}{3^{\cdots}}$ **iii** $8^{-7} = \dfrac{1}{8^{\cdots}}$ **iv** $7^{-3} = \dfrac{1}{7^{\cdots}}$

5 Write each calculation as a single power.

   a $5^3 \times 5^{-7} = 5^{3+(-7)} = 5^{\cdots}$ **b** $4^{-2} \times 4^5 = 4^{\cdots+\cdots} = 4^{\cdots}$ **c** 7×7^{-6} ....

   d $3^4 \div 3^9 = 3^{\cdots-\cdots} = 3^{\cdots}$ **e** $\dfrac{9^2}{9^{-5}}$ ....   **f** $(6^{-3})7 = 6^{\cdots\times\cdots} = 6^{\cdots}$

Standard form

6 Work out

   a 5.2×10^3 ....

   c 9.1×10^2 ....

   b 3.8×10^4 ....

   d 4.7×10^6 ....

> 5.2
> 5 2 0 0
> 5.2×10^3 means multiply 5.2 by 10 three times.

Guided

7 Work out

  a 6.5×10^{-3} ....

  b 2.7×10^{-4} ....

  c 8.3×10^{-2} ....

  d 9.4×10^{-6} ....

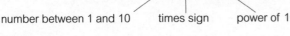

6.5 × 10⁻³ means divide 6.5 by 10 three times.

8 A number written in standard form looks like this:

$$A \times 10^{n}$$

number between 1 and 10   times sign   power of 10

Write each number using standard form.

  a $4900 = 4.9 \times 10^{......}$

  b $730\,000$ ....

  c $51\,000\,000\,000$ ....

9 Write each number using standard form.

  a $0.000\,83 = 8.3 \times 10^{......}$

  c 0.005 ....

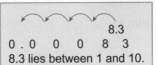

8.3 lies between 1 and 10.

  b $0.000\,009\,7$ ....

  d $0.000\,000\,004\,6$ ....

10 Jamila thinks that $3\,000\,000\,000$ is more than 3×10^{9}.

Is she correct? Explain your reasoning.

....

Calculating with standard form

11 Work out each calculation. Give your answers in standard form.

  a $(2.4 \times 10^{2}) \times (3 \times 10^{5})$

    $= 2.4 \times 3 \times 10^{2} \times 10^{5}$

    $= .... \times 10^{...}$

  b $(1.8 \times 10^{4}) \times (4 \times 10^{3})$

  c $(5 \times 10^{7}) \times (3.1 \times 10^{2})$

  d $\dfrac{8.4 \times 10^{7}}{2.1 \times 10^{2}}$

    $= \dfrac{8.4}{2.1} \times \dfrac{10^{7}}{10^{2}}$

    $= .... \times 10^{...}$

  e $\dfrac{7.2 \times 10^{5}}{6 \times 10^{8}}$

  f $\dfrac{4 \times 10^{11}}{5 \times 10^{7}}$

Worked example

1 **a** 1.03 cm = ...m

 b 3.35 g = ...mg

 c 72.6 ml = ...l

2 In this spider diagram, the four calculations give the answer in the middle.
Work out the missing numbers and complete the diagram.

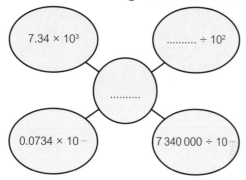

3 By rounding to 1 significant figure, estimate

 a 329 ÷ 96 = ...

 b 57 632 × 208 = ...

 c $\dfrac{62 \times 29}{196}$ = ...

4 Evaluate

 a $16(-2 + 4) + 3(6 - 9)^2$ = ...

 b $\dfrac{8(3)^7}{5 - 3} + 5^2$ = ...

 c $14 - \dfrac{9}{(-2 - 1)^2} + 3 \times 15$ = ...

5 **Reasoning** The area of a square is 3^8 cm^2.
What is the length of one side?
Write your answer as a power of 3.

....

3^8 cm^2

6 **Reasoning**

 a Circle the numbers with the same value?

 $(0.2)^3$ $\left(\dfrac{1}{2}\right)^3$ 5^{-3} $\left(\dfrac{1}{5}\right)^3$ 25^{-2}

 b Write $\dfrac{1}{100}$ in as many different ways as you can.

....

7 **Problem-solving** Write these numbers in order, from smallest to largest.

 3.17×10^{-4} 0.31×10^{-3} $0.000\,315$ 3106×10^{-7} $\dfrac{6.2 \times 10^{-9}}{2 \times 10^{-5}}$

Strategy hint

Write each number
in standard form first.

8 Work out the reciprocals of these numbers. Give your answers in standard form.

 a 2×10^7 **b** 5×10^6 **c** 8×10^{-4} **d** 2.5×10^{-6}

9 **Real** The populations of Austria, France, Italy, Switzerland and the UK are shown in the table.

 a Write these countries in order of population size, from smallest to largest.

Country	Population in 2014
Austria	8.53×10^6
France	6.605×10^7
Italy	6.078×10^7
Switzerland	8.18×10^6
UK	6.41×10^7

 b What is the difference between the populations of France and the UK?

 c Approximately how many times larger is the population of the UK than that of Austria?

 d What is the total population of these five countries?

The total population of Europe is 7.38×10^8.

 e What proportion of Europe's population lives in the UK or France?

10 **Problem-solving** In these multiplication pyramids, the number in a brick is the product of the two bricks below it.
Work out the missing entries. Write each answer in index form.

 a

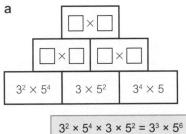

$3^2 \times 5^4 \times 3 \times 5^2 = 3^3 \times 5^6$

 b

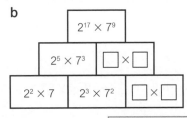

$2^5 \times 7^3 \times 2^{\square} \times 7^{\square} = 2^{17} \times 7^9$

11 **Reasoning** Use your answers from Q10 to help you complete these general rules.

 a $a^p \times b^q \times a^r \times b^s = a^{\,\cdots\cdots} \times b^{\,\cdots\cdots}$ **b** $\dfrac{a^p \times b^q}{a^r \times b^s} = a^{\,\cdots\cdots} \times b^{\,\cdots\cdots}$

1 Complete the table using the cards.

Prefix	Letter	Power	Number

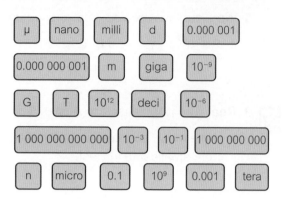

2 Estimate the answer to these calculations by rounding each number to 1 significant figure.

   a 765×38 ....

   b $4324 \div 53$ ....

3 Write as a single power.

   a $5^4 \times 5^{-11}$ ....

   b $8^{-3} \times 8^{-4}$ ....

   c $(3^{-2})^4$ ....

   d $\dfrac{6^{-5} \div 6^{-2}}{6^{-1} \times 6^{-3}}$ ....

4 Write each number in standard form.

   a 7900 ....

   b $0.000\,008\,13$ ....

5 The average distance of the Moon from the Earth is 3.84×10^5 km.

   Write this distance in metres as an ordinary number.

   ....

6 Work out each calculation. Give your answers in standard form.

   a $\dfrac{6.3 \times 10^9}{2.1 \times 10^5}$ ....

   b $(2.4 \times 10^5) \times (5 \times 10^{-11})$ ....

7 A bee has a mass of 1.2×10^{-4} kg. Write down the mass of the bee in grams.

8 A sheet of paper is 5×10^{-5} m thick. How many sheets of paper are there in an 801 cm tall stack of the same paper?

1 The diagram shows a triangular prism and its net.

Guided

a Write the missing lengths on the net.

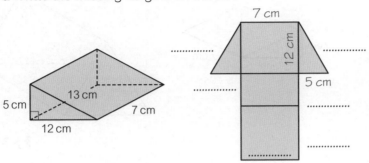

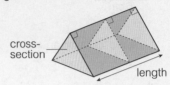

A prism is a solid with the same cross-section throughout its length. A right prism is a prism where the cross-section is at right angles to the length of the solid.

cross-section

length

The cross-section can be any flat shape.

Guided

b Calculate the area of each shape in the net.

Area of triangle $= \frac{1}{2}bh = \frac{1}{2} \times 12 \times 5 = $ .... cm²

c Calculate the total surface area of the prism.

2 For each solid **i** sketch the net **ii** calculate the total surface area.

a

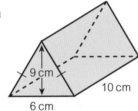

9 cm

10 cm

6 cm

b

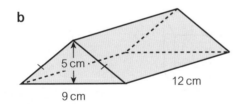

5 cm

12 cm

9 cm

3 **Problem-solving** These two solids have the same surface area. Work out the value of x.

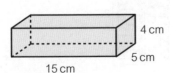

4 cm

5 cm

15 cm

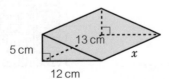

13 cm

5 cm

x

12 cm

Check Tick each box as your **confidence** in this topic improves.

🙁 😐 🙂

Need extra help? Go to page 17 and tick the boxes next to Q1 and 2. Then try them once you've finished 2.1–2.6.

11

Volume of prisms

1 For each triangular prism, work out   **i** the cross-sectional area   **ii** the volume.

a

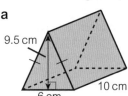

9.5 cm

10 cm

6 cm

b

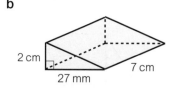

2 cm

27 mm

7 cm

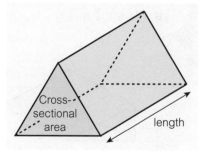

Cross-sectional area

length

i Area of a triangle $= \frac{1}{2}bh$
$= \frac{1}{2} \times 6 \times 9.5 = $ .... cm²

ii Volume = ... × 10 = ... cm³

Volume of a prism
= cross-sectional area × length

2 Calculate the volume of each prism.

a

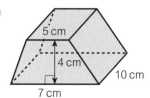

5 cm

4 cm

10 cm

7 cm

b

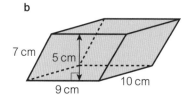

7 cm

5 cm

9 cm

10 cm

Worked example

3 The volume of this prism is 63 cm³.
Calculate the length marked x.

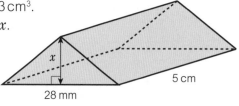

x

5 cm

28 mm

4 **Problem-solving** This pentagonal prism vase has a capacity of 420 m*l*.
The inside of the vase is 21 cm tall.

Capacity is the volume of liquid a 3D shape will hold.

a What is the area of the base of the inside of the tank?

The edges of the pentagon are each 5.5 cm long.

b What is the surface area of the inside of the vase?

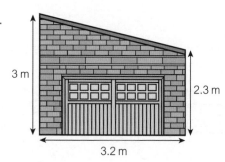

5 This is the vertical cross-section of a garage.

a Work out the area of the cross-section.

The length of the garage is 5 m.

b Calculate the volume of the garage.

3 m

2.3 m

3.2 m

Check

Tick each box as your **confidence** in this topic improves.

Need extra help? Go to page 17 and tick the box next to Q3. Then try it once you've finished 2.1–2.6.

12

1 Work out the circumference of each circle. Round your answers to 1 decimal place and include the units of measurement.

Guided

a

9 cm

$C = \pi d$

$= \pi \times \text{............}$

$= \text{............ } cm$

b

6.7 mm

The circumference (C) is the perimeter of a circle. The centre of a circle is marked using a dot. The radius (r) is the distance from the centre to the circumference. The diameter (d) is the distance from one edge to another through the centre. An arc is part of the circumference.

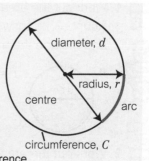

diameter, d

radius, r

centre

arc

circumference, C

The diameter is given, so use the formula $C = \pi d$.

2 STEM Calculate the circumference of each circular object. Round your answers to 1 decimal place.

a A 1p coin with diameter 20.3 mm. ....

b The London Eye with diameter 120 m. ....

c The Manicouagan Crater, the largest visible impact crater on Earth, with radius 50 km.

....

The Greek letter π (pronounced 'pi') is a special number, 3.141592653... To find the circumference, C, of a circle with diameter d, use the formula $C = \pi d$. If you know the radius, r, you can use the equivalent formula $C = 2\pi r$. Use the π key on your calculator.

3 For each circle work out

   i the circumference of the whole circle

   ii the fraction of the whole circle that is shaded

   iii the arc length of this part of the circle.
   Give your answers in terms of π.

a

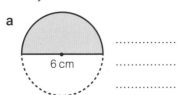

6 cm

....

....

....

b

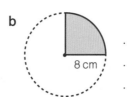

8 cm

....

....

....

4 For each shape, work out

   i the length of the arc   **ii** the perimeter of the whole shape.

a

2.3 cm

....

....

b

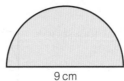

9 cm

....

....

The perimeter of a shape is the distance around the edge of the whole shape.

Worked example

5 A circle has circumference 35 cm. Work out its diameter. Round your answer to the nearest mm.

....

Strategy hint

Substitute the values into the formula and rearrange.

Check Tick each box as your **confidence** in this topic improves.

Need extra help? Go to page 17 and tick the boxes next to Q4–5. Then try them once you've finished 2.1–2.6.

1 Work out the area of each circle.
Round your answers to 1 decimal place
and include the units of measurement.

The formula for the area, A, of a
circle with radius r is $A = \pi r^2$

First work out the
radius of the circle.

**Worked
example**

a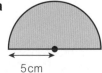

$r = $ .... cm

$A = \pi \times$ .... ^{2}

$= $ .... cm²

b

6.7 mm

2 Work out the area of each shape.
Give your answers in terms of π.

a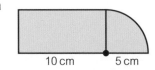

5 cm

b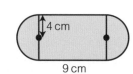

3.9 cm

c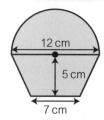

12.8 cm

3 Work out the area of each shape.
Round your answers to 1 decimal place.

Divide each shape up
into different parts.

a

10 cm   5 cm

b

4 cm

9 cm

c

12 cm

5 cm

7 cm

4 Work out the radius of this circle.
Round your answer to the nearest millimetre.

Area
72 cm²

$A = \pi r^2$
$72 = \pi \times r^2$
$r^2 = 72 \div \pi$
$r = \ldots$

5 Work out the shaded area of this shape.
Give your answer in terms of π.

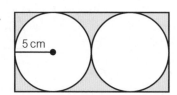

5 cm

Strategy hint

Work out the area of
the larger shape and
subtract the area of
the smaller shapes.

Check   Tick each box as your
confidence in this
topic improves.

Need extra help? Go to page 17 and tick
the boxes next to Q6–7. Then try them once
you've finished 2.1–2.6.

1 Work out the surface area of each cylinder.
Round your answers to 1 decimal place.

a

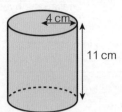

$A = 2\pi r^2 + 2\pi rh$

$\quad = 2 \times \pi \times \text{.....}^2 + 2 \times \pi \times \text{.....} \times \text{.....}$

$\quad = \text{................}$

> Surface area of a cylinder
> $= 2\pi r^2 + 2\pi rh$

b

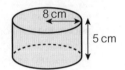

2 For each cylinder, work out

    i the area of the circular end   **ii** the volume of the cylinder.

Round your answers to 1 decimal place.

Volume of a cylinder $= \pi r^2 h$

a
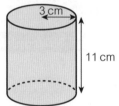

b
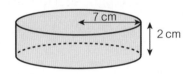

c
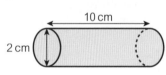

3 Modelling The inside of a cylindrical bucket has diameter 28 cm and height 43 cm.

  a Calculate the capacity of the bucket in cm³.

The manufacturer claims that the capacity of the bucket is 27 litres.

> 1 litre = 1000 cm³

  b Is the manufacturer's claim correct?
    Explain your answer.

4 Real / Problem-solving The recommended water intake for a 9- to 13-year-old
is 2.5 litres per day. Robyn has a cylindrical glass with diameter 6.5 cm and height 12 cm.
How many glasses of water should she drink each day?

Check   Tick each box as your
confidence in this
topic improves.   ☹ 😐 ☺

Need extra help? Go to page 18 and tick
the box next to Q8. Then try it once you've
finished 2.1–2.6.

15

Guided

1 Work out the length of the hypotenuse of each right-angled triangle.
Round your answers to the nearest mm.

> The longest side of a right-angled triangle is called the hypotenuse.

a

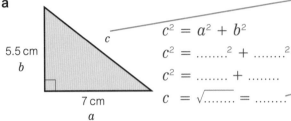

> Label the hypotenuse c and the other sides a and b.

$c^2 = a^2 + b^2$

$c^2 = \text{........}^2 + \text{........}^2$

$c^2 = \text{........} + \text{........}$

$c = \sqrt{\text{........}} = \text{........}$

> Substitute $a = 7$ and $b = 5.5$ into the formula for Pythagoras' theorem, $c^2 = a^2 + b^2$

> Use a calculator to find the square root. Round to the nearest mm.

b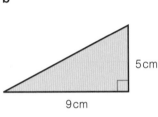

c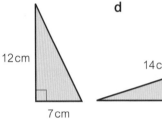

d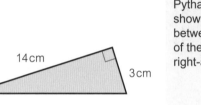

> Pythagoras' theorem shows the relationship between the lengths of the three sides of a right-angled triangle.

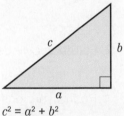

$c^2 = a^2 + b^2$

2 Problem-solving Work out which of these are right-angled triangles.

a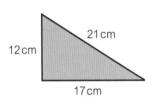

b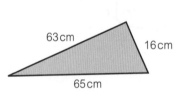

c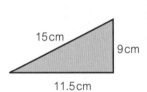

> **Strategy hint**
>
> First identify the hypotenuse of the triangle.
> If $c^2 = a^2 + b^2$, then the triangle is a right-angled triangle.

3 Work out the missing length in each right-angled triangle.
Round your answers to 1 decimal place.

a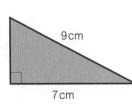

b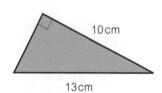

c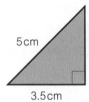

> **Strategy hint**
>
> Label the sides a, b and c.
> Substitute into Pythagoras' theorem $c^2 = a^2 + b^2$
> Solve the equation.

Guided

$$c^2 = a^2 + b^2$$
$$9^2 = 7^2 + b^2$$
$$81 - 49 = b^2$$
$$b = \sqrt{\text{........}} = \text{........}$$

4 Problem-solving Work out the area of this triangle.

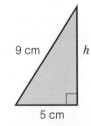

> Work out the height, h, first.

Check Tick each box as your **confidence** in this topic improves.

😦 😐 ☺

Need extra help? Go to page 18 and tick the boxes next to Q9–11. Then try them once you've finished 2.1–2.6.

16

Surface area and volume of prisms

1 Sketch the net of this triangular prism. Label all the lengths.

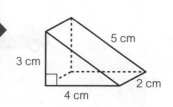

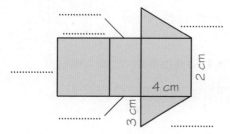

2 Work out the surface area of the triangular prism in Q1.

> Work out the area of each face and add them together.

> Volume = cross-sectional area × length.
>
>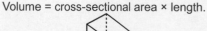
>
> You worked out the area of cross-section in Q2.

3 Work out the volume of the triangular prism in Q1.

Circumference and area of a circle

> *r* for radius

4 Write the length of the radius and diameter of each circle.

a 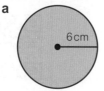 6cm $r =$ ....
                              $d =$ ....

b   11cm $r =$ ....
                              $d =$ ....

> *d* for diameter
>
>

5 Work out the circumference of each circle. Round your answers to 1 decimal place.

a   7.5cm $Circumference = \pi \times d = 2 \times \pi \times r$
                                      $= 2 \times \pi \times$ ....
                                      $=$ ....

b   6.2cm

6 a What is the radius of this circle? ....    7.6cm

  b Complete the formula for its area, *A*.

  $A = \pi \times$ .... ^{2}

> The area of a circle is $A = \pi \times radius^2$

  c Work out the area of the circle. Round your answer to 1 decimal place.

7 a What fraction of a circle is this shape? ....   8 cm

  b Work out the area of the whole circle. Give your answers in terms of π.

>

  c Work out the area of the sector shown.

> Use your answers to parts **a** and **b**.

  d Work out the circumference of the whole circle. Give your answers in terms of π.

> A sector is the part of a circle enclosed by two radii and an arc.
>
>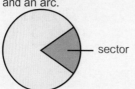
>
> sector

  e Work out the length of the arc.

  f Work out the perimeter of the sector.

> Radii is the plural of radius.

Cylinders

8 Here is a cylinder.

3 cm

7 cm

a Sketch its faces. Label the lengths you know.

Round all your answers to parts **b** to **e** to 1 decimal place.

b Work out the long length of the rectangle and label it.

c Work out the area of each face.

d Work out the total surface area of the cylinder.

e Work out the volume of the cylinder.

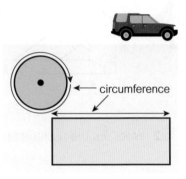

← circumference

Pythagoras' theorem

9 For each triangle

   i label the two shorter sides a and b, and label the hypotenuse c

   ii use the formula $c^2 = a^2 + b^2$ to find the length of the hypotenuse.
   Round your answers to 1 decimal place.

Worked example

a

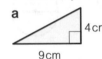

4 cm

9 cm

$c^2 = a^2 + b^2$
$c^2 = 4^2 + 9^2$

b

10 cm

6 cm

c

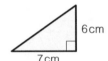

6 cm

7 cm

10 Work out the length of the missing side in each right-angled triangle.
   Round your answers to 1 decimal place.

a

12 cm

c

a

7 cm b

b

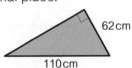

62 cm

110 cm

c

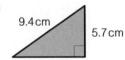

9.4 cm

5.7 cm

$c^2 = a^2 + b^2$

$12^2 = a^2 + 7^2$ ....

$a^2 = ...^2 - ....^2$

$a = \sqrt{........} = ...$

11 Work out the area of each shape.
   Round your answers to 1 decimal place.

Label the sides.
Use Pythagoras' theorem to first find the length labelled x.
Work out the area of the shape.

a

8 cm

x

5 cm

b

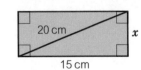

20 cm

15 cm

x

c

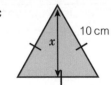

10 cm

x

1 Work out the perimeter of each shape.
Round your answers to the nearest millimetre.

First work out the arc length
of one semicircle.
Then work out the perimeter
of the whole shape.

a

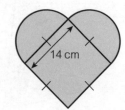

14 cm

b

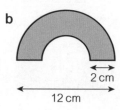

2 cm

12 cm

2 Here is a circle.
Alfie says, 'The circumference is 12π and the area is 36π.'

a Explain how he got his answers.

6 cm

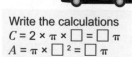

Write the calculations
$C = 2 \times \pi \times \square = \square \, \pi$
$A = \pi \times \square^2 = \square \, \pi$

b Now work out the circumference and area of this circle.
Leave your answer in terms of π, as in part **a**.

15 cm

To write an answer in terms of π
(pi), your answer should be $\square \, \pi$.
This gives an exact value for the
area or circumference.

3 A wheelchair designed for racing has two large rear
wheels and a smaller front wheel.
The radius of each rear wheel is 35 cm.

a i How far does the rear wheel travel in one revolution?
Give your answer in metres to 2 decimal places.

ii How many revolutions will it go through when racing 400 m?

Over the same distance, the front wheel rotates 254 times.

b i What is the circumference of the front wheel?
Give your answer in metres to 2 decimal places.

**Worked
example**

ii What is the radius of the front wheel?
Give your answer in centimetres to 1 decimal place.

4 a Find the radius of a circle with circumference 30 cm.

b Find the radius of a circle with area 45 cm².

5 The diagram shows a square-based pyramid.

   a Write the length of the distance x. ....

   b Use Pythagoras' theorem to calculate l, the slant height of the pyramid.

   c Calculate the area of one triangular face of the pyramid.

   d Calculate the area of the base of the pyramid.

   e Calculate the surface area of the pyramid.

   f Calculate the volume of the pyramid.

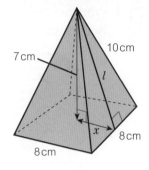

Volume of a pyramid = $\frac{1}{3}$ × area of base × height

6 **Problem-solving** Calculate the length of each of these lines.

Guided

   a AB

$$c^2 = a^2 + b^2$$
$$c^2 = 2^2 + 7^2$$
$$c = \sqrt{........}$$
$$ = ...$$

> Form a right-angled triangle.

> Use Pythagoras' theorem to calculate the distance between two points.

   b BC   **c** AC

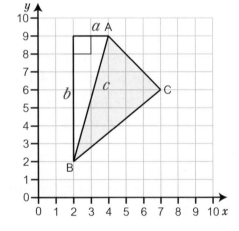

7 **Real** A cake recipe asks for a circular cake tin with diameter 20 cm and height 3 cm.
You only have a circular tin with diameter 12 cm and height 6 cm.
Will this tin be suitable? Show your working to explain.

8 Each cylinder has a volume of 1500 cm³.
Work out the missing length for each one. Round your answers to 2 decimal places.

   a 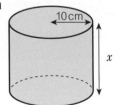   **b**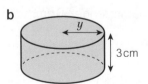

1 For each circle, work out **i** the circumference **ii** the area.

a
4 cm

b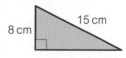
65 mm

Give your answers in terms of π.

 2 Work out the missing length in each triangle.

a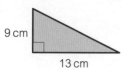
9 cm
13 cm

b
15 cm
8 cm

 3 For each prism, work out **i** the volume **ii** the surface area.

a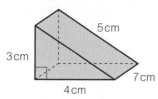
5 cm
3 cm
7 cm
4 cm

b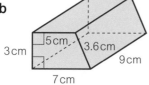
5 cm
3 cm
3.6 cm
9 cm
7 cm

 4 Work out the area of this triangle.

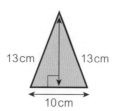
13 cm   13 cm
10 cm

 5 For this cylinder, work out

a the volume

b the surface area.

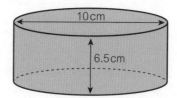
10 cm
6.5 cm

1 Write whether each sequence is arithmetic or quadratic.

> An **arithmetic** sequence goes up or down in equal steps.

a 1, 4, 7, 10, 13, ...

b 1, 4, 9, 16, 25, ...

> An nth term that includes n^2 (and no higher power of n) generates a quadratic sequence.

c 13, 8, 3, −2, −7, ...

Guided

2 Work out the first four terms and the 10th term of the quadratic sequence with

> $T(n)$ is another way of writing the nth term.

a $T(n) = n^2$

First four terms: 1,.......... ,.......... ,..........

> $T(1) = 1^2 = 1$
> $T(2) = 2^2 = \square$

b $T(n) = 2n^2$

10th term: ....

c $T(n) = -3n^2$

d $T(n) = 5n^2$

3 **Reasoning** Find the 5th and 10th terms of the sequence $T(n) = 2n^2 + 3$.
Explain why the 10th term is not double the 5th term.

4 Work out the first four terms and the 10th term for each quadratic sequence.

a $T(n) = n^2 + 5$

....

b $T(n) = 2n^2 + 5$

....

c $T(n) = 3n^2 + 5$

....

5 The first two terms of an arithmetic sequence are 3, 8, ...

> The sequence is arithmetic, so it goes up or down in equal steps.

a Write down the next three terms.

....

b What is the common difference?

> The common difference is what you add or subtract to find the next term.

....

c What is the nth term of the sequence?

....

d What is the relationship between the common difference and the nth term of the sequence?

....

....

Check Tick each box as your **confidence** in this topic improves.

Need extra help? Go to page 27 and tick the boxes next to Q1 and 3. Then try them once you've finished 3.1–3.5.

22

1 Find the next three terms of the geometric sequences that start

   a 1, 4, ...

     $4 \div 1 = 4$

     3rd term $= 4 \times 4 = 16$ 4th term $= 16 \times 4 =$ ....   5th term $=$ .... $\times$ .... $=$ ....

   b 2, 8, ...

> To work out the common ratio, divide the 2nd term by the 1st term.
> $4 \div 1 = ...$
> Then multiply each term by the common ratio.

   c 625, 125, ...

   d 5000, 500, ...

2 Complete the sentence with either 'ascending' or 'descending'.

   If the common ratio of a geometric sequence is greater than 1, the sequence is ....

   If the common ratio of a geometric sequence is between 0 and 1, the sequence is ....

3 **Problem-solving** The first two terms of a geometric sequence are 0.2 and 2.

   a Work out the common ratio. ....

   b How many terms are smaller than 500? ....

4 Write down the first five terms of the geometric sequence with

   a first term $= 2$ common ratio $= 5$

   b first term $= 100$ common ratio $= \frac{1}{2}$

   c first term $= 1$ common ratio $= -2$

   d first term $= 200$ common ratio $= 0.2$

Check Tick each box as your **confidence** in this topic improves. ☹ 😐 ☺   **Need extra help?** Go to page 27 and tick the box next to Q2. Then try it once you've finished 3.1–3.5.

23

1 Expand and simplify

a $(x + 4)(x + 3)$

$= x^2 + 3x + 4x + 12$

$= x^2 + 7x + 12$

$(x + 4)(x + 3) = x^2 + 3x + 4x + 12$

$= x^2 + 7x + 12$

When you **expand** double brackets, you multiply each term in one set of brackets by each term in the other set of brackets. $(a + b)(c + d) = ac + ad + bc + bd$

b $(y + 2)(y + 7)$ **c** $(a + 3)(a + 5)$ **d** $(p + 6)(p + 4)$ **e** $(n + 7)(n + 8)$

2 Expand and simplify

a $(d + 4)(d - 5)$ **b** $(z + 5)(z - 6)$ **c** $(q - 2)(q + 5)$

d $(b - 3)(b - 7)$ **e** $(f - 8)(f - 4)$ **f** $(b - 9)(b - 5)$

Be careful with negative numbers. $-3 \times -7 = +21$

3 **Problem-solving / Reasoning** Dan and Emily both expand and simplify the quadratic expression $(x - 5)(-6 + x)$.
Dan says the answer is $x^2 - 11x + 30$.
Emily says the answer is $x^2 + x - 30$.
Only one of them is correct. Who is it? What mistakes were made?

4 Expand and simplify

a $(x + 5)(x - 7) + x(3x - 1)$

Expand $(x + 5)(x - 7)$.
Expand $x(3x - 1)$.
Add them together.

b $(x - 4)^2 - 5(x + 6)$ $(x - 4)^2 = (x - 4)(x - 4)$

5 **Problem-solving / Reasoning** Show that $x(x - 10) + 9(x + 1) = (x - 3)(x - 4) + 3(2x - 1)$.

6 Expand the double brackets and simplify where possible.

a $(2x + 5)(x - 3)$ **b** $(3x - 4)(2x - 5)$ **c** $(2x - 3)(5x + 1)$

Follow the same rules as you did in Q1, 2 and 3.

7 Expand and simplify

a $(2x + 1)^2$ **b** $(3x + 2)^2$ **c** $(5x - 3)^2$ **d** $(6x - 7)^2$

Worked example

8 Expand and simplify

a $(2x + 3)(2x - 3)$ **b** $(3x + 1)(3x - 1)$ **c** $(5x + 2)(5x - 2)$ **d** $(x + y)(x - y)$

Check Tick each box as your **confidence** in this topic improves. ☹ 😐 ☺

Need extra help? Go to pages 27 and 28 and tick the boxes next to Q4–7. Then try them once you've finished 3.1–3.5.

24

Factorising

Guided

1 Factorise each quadratic expression. Check your answers.

a $x^2 + 5x + 6 = (x + 2)(x + 3)$

$2 + 3 \quad 2 \times 3$

> The **factor pairs** of 6 are 1 × 6 and 2 × 3. Only the 2 and 3 add together to make 5 so these are the numbers that go in the brackets.

Check: $(x + 2)(x + 3) = x^2 + 3x + 2x + 2 \times 3$
$= x^2 + 5x + 6$

> Check your answer by expanding.

> Remember that −1 × −7 = 7 as well as 1 × 7 = 7.

b $x^2 + 8x + 15$ **c** $x^2 + 13x + 22$ **d** $x^2 - 8x + 7$ **e** $x^2 - 10x + 24$

2 Factorise each quadratic expression. Check your answers.

a $x^2 + 3x - 10$ **b** $x^2 + x - 12$ **c** $x^2 + 7x - 18$

d $x^2 - 5x - 24$ **e** $x^2 - 8x - 20$ **f** $x^2 + 3x - 28$

> **Worked example**
>
>

Guided

3 Write these as perfect squares.

a $x^2 + 10x + 25 = x^2 + 2ax + a^2$

$(x + \ldots)^2$

> What value of a squares to give 25 and doubles to give 10?

> A **perfect square** is of the form
> $(x + a)^2 = (x + a)(x + a) = x^2 + 2ax + a^2$

b $x^2 + 8x + 16$ **c** $x^2 - 18x + 81$ **d** $x^2 - 14x + 49$

4 Factorise each quadratic expression. Check your answers.

a $x^2 - 9$ **b** $x^2 - 4$ **c** $x^2 - 36$

> The middle term has cancelled out when collecting like terms.

5 **Problem-solving** The area of a rectangle is $x^2 + 15x + 56$.
What could the side lengths of the rectangle be?

6 **Problem-solving** Yuto adjusts the sides of a rectangle so that its perimeter remains the same and its new area is $x^2 - 25$.

a How did he change the two sides?   **b** Describe the original shape.

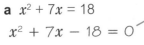

1 Solve each quadratic equation by factorising.

Check your answers.

You can solve some quadratic equations by setting them equal to 0 and factorising.

a $x^2 + 7x = 18$

$x^2 + 7x - 18 = 0$ — Rearrange the equation so it equals 0.

$(x + 9)(x - 2) = 0$ — Factorise the quadratic expression.

$x + 9 = 0 \quad x = -9$

$x - 2 = 0 \quad x = 2$ — 0 multiplied by any number is 0. So either $x + 9 = 0$ or $x - 2 = 0$.

$x = -9 \text{ or } x = 2$

Check by substitution:

$x = -9$

$(-9)^2 + (7 \times -9) = 81 - 63 = 18$ ✓

$x = 2$

$(2)^2 + (7 \times 2) = 4 + 14 = 18$ ✓

b $x^2 - 10x = 24$ **c** $x^2 - 13x = -36$ **d** $x^2 - x = 42$

2 Solve each quadratic equation by factorising. Check your answers by substitution.

a $x^2 + 12x = -36$ **b** $x^2 + 18x = -81$ **c** $x^2 - 8x = -16$

3 **Problem-solving** Jehaan is 5 years older than her brother Chavdar. The product of their ages is 234. How old is each of them?

4 **Problem-solving** The square of a number is equal to 36 less than 15 times the number. Work out two possible values for the number.

5 Solve these equations to work out x.

a $x^2 + 11 = 27$ **b** $x^2 - 18 = 46$ **c** $x^2 - 45 = 55$

Check   Tick each box as your **confidence** in this topic improves.

Need extra help? Go to page 29 and tick the boxes next to Q11–13. Then try them once you've finished 3.1–3.5.

3
Strengthen

Arithmetic, quadratic and geometric sequences

☐ **1** Are these arithmetic sequences? Write 'Yes' or 'No'.

a 5   10   16   23 …   …………………

+5   +6   +7

> In an arithmetic sequence the difference between consecutive terms is constant.

b 5, 10, 15, 20, …   …………………

c 5, 10, 20, 40, …   …………………

☐ **2** Are these geometric sequences? Write 'Yes' or 'No'.

a 2, 20, 200, 2000, …   …………………

b 5000, 500, 50, 5, …   …………………

c 500, 550, 600, 650, …   …………………

> In a geometric sequence the ratio between consecutive terms is constant.
> $20 \div 2$ $= …$
> $200 \div 20$ $= …$
> $2000 \div 200 = …$

☐ **3** Work out the first four terms and the 10th term of each quadratic sequence.

> 1st term: $T(1) = 1^2$
> 2nd term: $T(2) = 2^2$

a $T(n) = n^2$

……………………………………………………………………………………………

b $T(n) = n^2 + 1$

……………………………………………………………………………………………

c $T(n) = n^2 + 2$

……………………………………………………………………………………………

d $T(n) = 2n^2$

……………………………………………………………………………………………

e $T(n) = 3n^2$

……………………………………………………………………………………………

Expanding

☐ **4** Expand and simplify.

a $(x + 6)(x + 4)$

×	×	+6
×	$+x^2$	$+6x$
+4	$-4x$	$+24$

Answer: $x^2 + 6x + 4x + 24$

Simplify: $x^2 +$ ……… $+$ ………

b $(x + 3)(x + 7)$

c $(x + 5)(x + 1)$

d $(x + 8)(x - 3)$

×	×	+8
×		
−3	$-3x$	-24

e $(x - 5)(x - 9)$

f $(x - 6)(x - 2)$

5 Expand and simplify

   a $(x + 6)^2$ **b** $(x - 8)^2$ **c** $(x + 1)^2$

$(x + 6)^2 = (x + 6)(x + 6)$

6 Expand and simplify

   a $(x + 6)(x - 6)$ **b** $(x - 8)(x + 8)$ **c** $(x + y)(x - y)$

Look at what happens to the middle two terms.

7 Expand and simplify

   a $(2x + 3)(x - 4)$ **b** $(3x + 5)(4x - 1)$ **c** $(x - 7)(2x - 1)$

$2x \times x = 2x^2$
$3x \times 4x = 3 \times x \times 4 \times x$
$= 12 \times x^2$
$= 12x^2$

Factorising

8 a Which two numbers

   i add together to make 12 and multiply to make 35 ....

   ii add together to make 8 and multiply to make 12? ....

 b Factorise each quadratic expression.
   Check your answers by expanding the brackets.

   i $x^2 + 12x + 35 = (x + \ldots\ldots)(x + \ldots\ldots)$

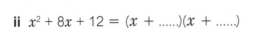

Use your answer to part **a i**.

Worked example

   ii $x^2 + 8x + 12 = (x + \ldots\ldots)(x + \ldots\ldots)$ **iii** $x^2 + 9x + 20$ ....

   iv $x^2 + 13x + 30$ ....   **v** $x^2 + 10x + 9$ ....

9 a Which two numbers add together to make -7 and multiply to make 10? ....

 b Factorise each quadratic expression.
   i $x^2 - 7x + 10 = (x - \ldots\ldots)(x - \ldots\ldots)$

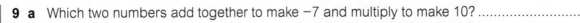

negative × negative = positive
negative + negative = negative

   ii $x^2 - 10x + 16 = (x - \ldots\ldots)(x - \ldots\ldots)$ **iii** $x^2 - 11x + 30$ ....

10 Factorise

   a $x^2 - 8x - 20$ **b** $x^2 - 3x - 28$ **c** $x^2 - 8x - 33$

> negative × positive = negative
> negative + positive = positive
> or negative

   d $x^2 + 3x - 18$ **e** $x^2 + 2x - 24$ **f** $x^2 + x - 42$ **g** $x^2 + 21x - 72$

Solving quadratic equations

11 Solve each quadratic equation by factorising.

   a $x^2 + 4x = -3$

      $x^2 + 4x + 3 = 0$ > Rearrange the equation so it equals zero. Add 3 to both sides of the equation.

      $(x + 3)(x + 1) = 0$ > Factorise the left-hand side.

      $x + 3 = 0$ or $x + 1 = 0$ > The solutions are the values that make either bracket zero.

      $x = -3$ or $x = -1$

   b $x^2 + 11x = -24$

   c $x^2 + 4x = 12$ **d** $x^2 - 12x = 28$ **e** $x^2 + 14x = -45$

   f $x^2 - 3x = 10$ **g** $x^2 + 10x = -25$ **h** $x^2 - 2x = 48$

12 Problem-solving The length of a rectangle is 5 cm more than its width. The area is 84 cm². Find the length and the width of the rectangle.

> Let the width of the rectangle be x.
> Create an expression for the length of the rectangle in terms of x.
> Form an equation for the area of the rectangle.
> Factorise and solve the equation.

13 Problem-solving Alfie is 3 years older than his brother Ben. Their ages multiplied together make 208.

   a How old is Alfie?

   b How old is Ben?

1 Work out the first four terms, the 50th term and the 100th term of each sequence.

a $T(n) = n^2 + 4n - 2$ **b** $T(n) = 2n^2 + 3n - 5$ **c** $T(n) = -4n^2 + 5n - 2$

> Substitute the term number into the expression.

2 Reasoning / Problem-solving The first two terms of a sequence are $\frac{1}{4}$ and $\frac{1}{2}$.

Write down the 5th term of the sequence if it is

a arithmetic ....

b geometric. ....

3 Problem-solving / Modelling A post on a social media website has received these numbers of comments. Predict how many comments the post will have after 7 days.

Day	1	2	3	4
Number of comments	225	450	775	1200

4 Expand and simplify the two sets of double brackets.

Guided

a $(x + 4)(x + 7) - (x + 8)(x + 5)$

$= (x^2 + 7x + 4x + 28) - (x^2 + 5x + 8x + 40)$ — Expand each set of double brackets.

$= (x^2 + 11x + 28) - (x^2 + 13x + 40)$ — Simplify each set of brackets.

$= x^2 + 11x + 28 - x^2 - 13x - 40$ — Multiply the second set of brackets by −1.

$= -2x - 12$ — Simplify.

$= -2(x + 6)$

b $(x + 6)(x + 7) - (x + 9)(x + 4)$ **c** $(x + 12)(x - 2) - (x - 3)(x + 7)$

5 Expand and simplify the three sets of brackets.

Guided

a $(x + 3)(x + 5)(x + 1)$

$(x + 3)(x + 5) = x^2 + 5x + 3x + 15 = x^2 + 8x + 15$ — First expand the first two sets of brackets.

$(x + 1)(x^2 + 8x + 15) = x^3 + 8x^2 + 15x + x^2 + 8x + 15$ — Then multiply the expression you get by the third set of brackets.

$= x^3 + 9x^2 + 23x + 15$

b $(x + 4)(x + 3)(x - 2)$ **c** $(x - 5)(x + 2)(x - 4)$

6 Factorise each quadratic expression.
The first two have been started for you.

    a $2x^2 - 7x + 3 = (2x - ....)(x - ....)$

    b $3x^2 + 4x - 4 = (3x - ....)(x + ...)$

    c $3x^2 + 2x - 5 ....$

    d $-2x^2 - 5x + 12 ....$

    e $-5x^2 + 17x - 6 ....$

    f $-5x^2 + 24x + 5 ....$

7 Factorise each quadratic expression.

    a $4x^2 - x - 3$ **b** $4x^2 - 4x - 3$ **c** $9x^2 - 4$

> The factor pairs of $4x^2$ are x and $4x$, $2x$ and $2x$, $-x$ and $-4x$, and $-2x$ and $-2x$.

    d $9x^2 + 12x - 5$ **e** $12x^2 - 16x - 3$ **f** $12x^2 + x - 6$

8 **Problem-solving** The area of a rectangular picture is $6x^2 - 11x - 10$.
Write down expressions for the length and the width of the picture.

9 Solve

    a $4x^2 + 4x = 15$ **b** $6x^2 + 19x = -10$ **c** $10x^2 + 11x = 6$

10 **Problem-solving** Jin thinks of a number.
He squares it, then subtracts 24.
His answer is twice the original number.
What is his number?

> Start by forming an equation for the number.

11 Solve each equation by factorising.

    a $x^2 + 8x = -7$ **b** $x^2 + 12x = -11$ **c** $x^2 + 22x + 21 = 0$

1 An arithmetic sequence starts 10, 12, …

   a Write down the next three terms in the sequence.

   ....

   b Write down the nth term of the sequence. ....

2 Expand and simplify

   a $(x + 5)(x + 1)$ **b** $(x + y)(x + y)$ **c** $(x + 6)(x - 4)$ **d** $(x + y)(x - y)$

3 Expand and simplify

   a $(x + 7)^2$ **b** $(x + y)^2$ **c** $(x - 3)^2$ **d** $(x - y)^2$

4 The 2nd and 3rd terms of a geometric sequence are 1 and 5.

   Write down the

   a 4th term ....   **b** 1st term. ....

5 Expand and simplify

   a $(2x - 5)(x + 6)$ **b** $(3x - 7)(x - 2)$ **c** $(4x + 3)(3x - 2)$

6 Factorise

   a $x^2 + 3x - 40$ **b** $x^2 + x - 12$ **c** $x^2 - 4x - 21$

7 Factorise

   a $x^2 - 64$ **b** $x^2 - y^2$

   c $25x^2 - 121$ **d** $x^2 + 6x + 9$

8 Solve

   a $x^2 - 2x = 63$ **b** $x^2 + 9x = -18$ **c** $x^2 + 9x = 10$

1 Construct each triangle PQR.

a PQ = 8 cm, QR = 7 cm and PR = 6 cm

6 cm   8 cm

Sketch the triangle first.

7 cm

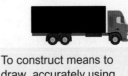

Worked example

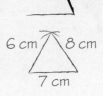

To construct means to draw accurately using a ruler and compasses.

1 Sketch the triangle first.
2 Draw a 7 cm line.
3 Open your compasses to 6 cm. Place the point at one end of the 7 cm line. Draw an arc.
4 Open your compasses to 8 cm. Draw an arc from the other end of the 7 cm line. Make sure your arcs are long enough to intersect.
5 Join the intersection of the arcs to each end of the 7 cm line.
Don't rub out your construction marks.

6 cm   8 cm

7 cm

7 cm

b PQ = 6.2 cm, QR = 5.5 cm and PR = 4.9 cm

c PQ = 7.6 cm, QR = 8.5 cm and PR = 5.3 cm

2 Three shapes join together to form a regular tetrahedron.
   Use a ruler and compasses to construct a net of the completed shape.

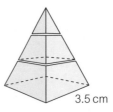

3.5 cm

Check   Tick each box as your **confidence** in this topic improves.   ☹ 😐 ☺

Need extra help? Go to pages 36 and 37 and tick the boxes next to Q1–5. Then try them once you've finished 4.1–4.3.

33

1 Draw a straight line 6 cm long.
Construct its perpendicular bisector.

A perpendicular bisector cuts a line in half at right angles.

Guided

6 cm

1 Use a ruler to draw the line.

2 Open your compasses to more than half the length of the line.

3 Place the point on one end of the line and draw an arc above and below.

4 Keeping the compasses open to the same distance, move the point to the other end of the line and draw a similar arc.

5 Join the points where the arcs intersect. Don't rub out your construction marks.
This line is the perpendicular bisector.

2 a Draw a straight line AB 10 cm long.
Mark the point P on AB 6 cm from A.

   b Follow these steps to construct a line through P that is perpendicular to AB.

   i Open your compasses to less than the distance PB.

   ii Put the point of the compasses at point P.

   iii Draw two arcs centred on P. Label them Q and R.

   iv Open your compasses a little more.

   v Construct the perpendicular bisector of QR.

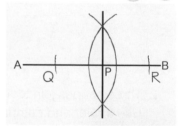

Worked example

Check Tick each box as your **confidence** in this topic improves.

Need extra help? Go to pages 38 and 39 and tick the boxes next to Q6 and 9. Then try them once you've finished 4.1–4.3.

Constructions 2

1 Draw an angle of 60°.
Construct the angle bisector.

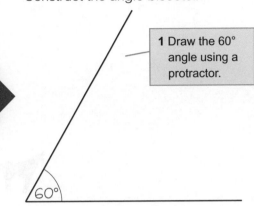

1 Draw the 60° angle using a protractor.

2 Open your compasses and place the point at the vertex of the angle.
Draw an arc that cuts both arms of the angle.

3 Keep the compasses open to the same distance. Move them to one of the points where the arc crosses the arms.

4 Make an arc in the middle of the angle. Do the same from the point where the arc crosses the other arm.

5 Join the vertex of the angle to the point where the two small arcs intersect.
Don't rub out your construction marks.
This line is the angle bisector.

2 Bisect each angle using a ruler and compasses.

a

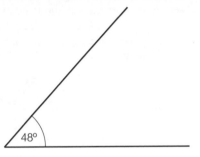

48°

b

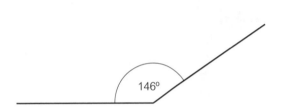

146°

3 Use a ruler and compasses to construct this parallelogram.

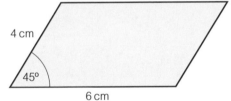

4 cm

45°

6 cm

Start by bisecting a line to construct a right angle.

Check Tick each box as your **confidence** in this topic improves.

Need extra help? Go to pages 38 and 39 and tick the boxes next to Q7, 8 and 10. Then try them once you've finished 4.1–4.3. 35

Constructing shapes

☐ **1** Construct a triangle with sides 6 cm, 8 cm and 7 cm.

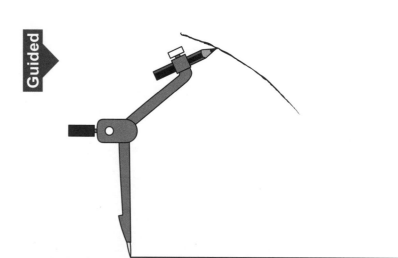

Use a ruler to draw the 8 cm side accurately. The 6 cm side starts at the left-hand end of this line. Open your compasses to exactly 6 cm and draw an arc from the left-hand end of the line.

Open your compasses to exactly 7 cm and draw an arc from the other end.

Use the point where the arcs cross to create the finished triangle.

☐ **2** Construct this triangle.

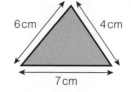

6 cm   4 cm

7 cm

3 Construct a scale diagram of this triangle.
Use a scale of 1 cm to 1 m.

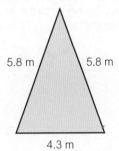

5.8 m   5.8 m

4.3 m

4 Draw and construct an accurate net of this triangular prism.

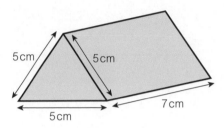

5 cm   5 cm

5 cm   7 cm

5 Sketch and then construct an accurate net of this
square-based pyramid.

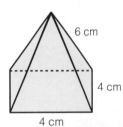

6 cm

4 cm

4 cm

**Worked
example**

Strategy hint

Sketch the net and write
the measurements on it.
Make an accurate drawing
of the square using a ruler
and protractor.
Construct the triangles
using compasses.

4
Strengthen

Constructions

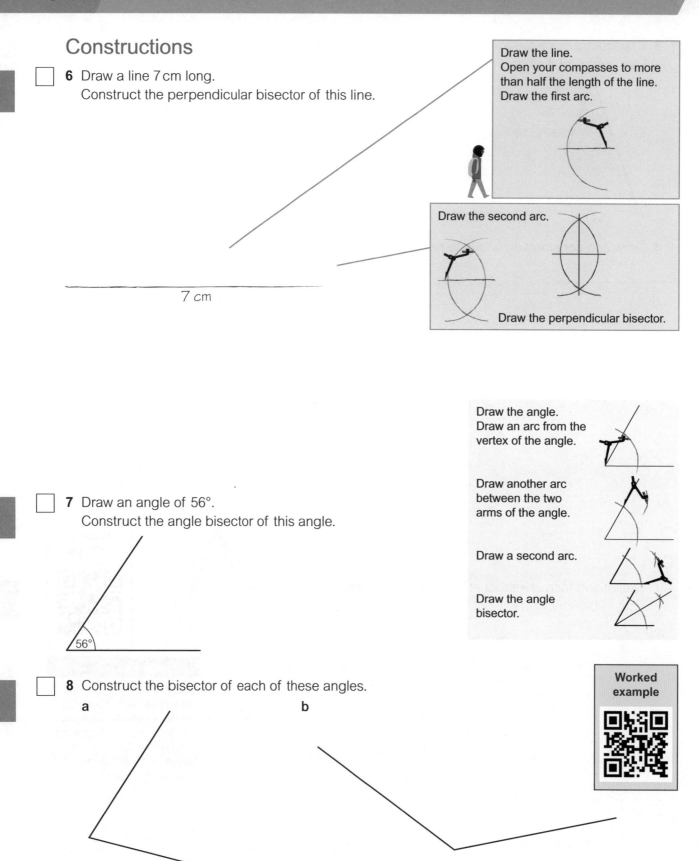

6 Draw a line 7 cm long.
   Construct the perpendicular bisector of this line.

Draw the line.
Open your compasses to more than half the length of the line.
Draw the first arc.

Draw the second arc.

Draw the perpendicular bisector.

7 cm

7 Draw an angle of 56°.
   Construct the angle bisector of this angle.

56°

Draw the angle.
Draw an arc from the vertex of the angle.

Draw another arc between the two arms of the angle.

Draw a second arc.

Draw the angle bisector.

8 Construct the bisector of each of these angles.
   a   b

Worked example

9 a Construct the perpendicular bisector of the line AB.

  b i Choose a point on the perpendicular bisector.

    ii Measure its distance from A and from B. ....

    iii Do this again for another point on the perpendicular bisector. What do you notice?

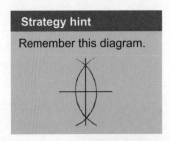

A ————————————————— B

10 a Draw the angle bisector of this angle.

  b i Choose a point on the angle bisector.

    ii Measure its shortest distance from each of the two lines. ....

    iii Do this again for another point on the angle bisector. What do you notice?

Use a protractor to measure the two smaller angles. What do you notice?

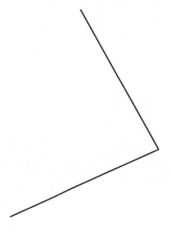

1 Reasoning

  a Construct triangle ABC where AB = 5.5 cm, BC = 6.5 cm and AC = 7.5 cm.

  b Construct the perpendicular bisectors of AB and BC.
    Mark the point P where they cross.

  c Construct the perpendicular bisector of AC.
    What do you notice?

  d Draw accurately a circle with
    centre P and radius PC.
    What do you notice?

2 Problem-solving / Reasoning The diagram shows a hexagonal pyramid.
  The base is a regular hexagon.
  Construct the net of a hexagonal pyramid using a ruler and compasses.

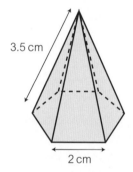

3.5 cm

2 cm

Hexagonal base:

Sketch one face. What type
of triangle are the faces?

3 a Construct this triangle.

   b Measure the hypotenuse. ....

   c Use Pythagoras' theorem to check your answer.

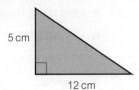

5 cm

12 cm

4 a Construct an isoceles triangle PQR where PQ = PR = 8 cm and angle QPR = 45°.

   b Measure and write the length of QR. ....

First draw a sketch of the triangle. Construct a right angle and bisect it to construct an angle of 45°.

5 Problem-solving Use a ruler and compasses to construct an angle of 75°. Check your angle using a protractor.

How does 75° relate to angles you know, such as 60° and 90°?

Worked example

1 a Use a protractor to draw an angle of 70°.

   b Construct the angle bisector.

2 Use a ruler and compasses to construct an angle of 45°.

3 a Draw a line AB of length 8 cm.

   b Construct the perpendicular bisector of AB.

   c Draw accurately the circle that passes through A and B.

   d Choose any point P on the circumference of the circle. Measure angle APB.

4 Sketch and then construct an accurate net of this triangular prism.

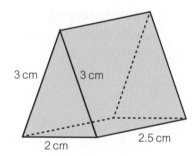

3 cm   3 cm

2 cm   2.5 cm

1 Work out the value of each expression when $a = 3$, $b = 5$ and $c = -2$.

a $a^2 + 2b - 3c$

$a^2 + 2b - 3c = 3^2 + 2 \times \ldots - \ldots \times (-2) =$

b $(2a + b)^2 - 3c$

c $9a^2 + (b + c)^2$

2 An online book shop charges \$4.20 per book plus a one off cost of \$10.00 for shipping any number of books.

a How much would it cost to buy 3 books?

b Write a formula to calculate the cost (C) of n books.

c Mali's books cost \$39.40. How many books did she buy?

3 The formula for calculating density is $d = \dfrac{m}{v}$

where m = mass in g, v = volume in cm³ and d is density in g/cm³.

Work out

a d if $m = 7$ g and $v = 5$ cm³

b m if $d = 8$ g/cm³ and $v = 4$ cm³

c v if $m = 10$ g and $d = 12$ g/cm³.

Guided

1 a Show these inequalities on a number line.

i $-2 \leqslant x < 4$

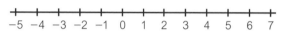

> This includes all the numbers less than 4 (excluding 4) and greater than or equal to −2 (including −2).

> You can show **inequalities** on a number line.
> An empty circle ○ shows that the value is not included.
> A filled circle ● shows that the value is included.
> An arrow ○→ shows that the solution continues to plus or minus infinity.

ii $x > -1$

iii $-3 < x \leqslant 2$

iv $-3 \leqslant x \leqslant 5$

> You can solve inequalities in a similar way to solving equations.

Guided

b Solve these inequalities. Show each solution on a number line.

i $x + 5 \leqslant 12$

$x \leqslant 12 - 5$

> Subtract 5 from both sides.

$x \leqslant 7$

ii $\dfrac{x}{3} > -2$

iii $3x - 7 \leqslant 8$

> **Worked example**

2 STEM In a kitchen experiment, Cabir mixes diet cola and mint sweets to make a 'geyser' eruption (explosion). He uses 500 ml of diet cola.
In order to get the geyser to erupt (explode), Cabir must use x sweets, where $125x \leqslant 500$.

a Solve the inequality.

b Connor has 3 sweets. Does this satisfy the inequality?

3 Solve these inequalities.

Guided

a $-9 \leqslant 2x - 1 < 5$

$-9 + 1 \leqslant 2x < 5 + 1$

$-8 \leqslant 2x < 6$

$\dfrac{-8}{2} \leqslant x < \dfrac{6}{2}$

.... $\leqslant x <$ ....

b $-9 < 4y + 3 \leqslant 19$

c $-23 < 3z - 5 \leqslant 7$

4 Solve these inequalities.

a $-x > 4$

b $10 - x \leqslant 3$

c $-6 < -x < 14$

> $-x$ is greater than 4, so x is less than ☐.

Check Tick each box as your **confidence** in this topic improves. ☹ 😐 🙂

Need extra help? Go to page 49 and tick the boxes next to Q2–4. Then try them once you've finished 5.1–5.6.

1 Reasoning Write down the value of

   a 1^0 ....   **b** 2^0 ....   **c** 5^0 ....   **d** x^0 ....   **e** $2m^0$ ....

> Any number to the power of zero is 1.
>
> $x^0 = 1$ and $y^0 = 1$

2 Work out the value of each expression.

   a $5x^0 + 7y^0$ **b** $9a^0 \times 4b^0$

   c $\dfrac{42}{7p^0}$ **d** $15c^0 - \dfrac{4^2}{2d^0}$

3 Simplify these expressions. Write each one as a negative power and as a fraction.

   a $\dfrac{x^3}{x^8} = x^{3-8} = x^{\cdots} = \dfrac{1}{x^{\cdots}}$ **b** $\dfrac{p^5}{p^9}$

   c $\dfrac{n^4}{n^{11}}$ **d** $\dfrac{h}{h^7}$ $h = h^1$

4 Simplify these expressions.
Write each one as

   i a negative power   **ii** a fraction.

   a $\dfrac{10a^5}{2a^8}$

      i $\dfrac{10a^5}{2a^8} = \dfrac{10}{2} \times \dfrac{a^5}{a^8}$ ——— Write the fraction as the product of two simpler fractions.

      $\dfrac{10}{2} \times \dfrac{a^5}{a^8} =$ ——— Simplify the two fractions.
$10 \div 2 = 5$
$\dfrac{a^5}{a^8} = a^{5-8} = a^{-3}$

      $5 \times a^{-3} = 5a^{-3}$ ——— A negative power as a fraction is 1 over the positive power.
$a^{-3} = \dfrac{1}{a^3}$

      ii $5a^{-3} = 5 \times \dfrac{1}{a^3} = \dfrac{5}{a^3}$

   b $\dfrac{56m^4}{8m^9}$ **c** $\dfrac{35t}{7t^9}$ **d** $\dfrac{9e^7}{36e^{12}}$ **e** $\dfrac{6v}{42v^{12}}$

5 Simplify these expressions.

   a $\dfrac{12x^3}{3x^3}$ **b** $\dfrac{18x^5}{6x^5}$ **c** $\dfrac{6x^2}{24x^2}$ **d** $\dfrac{5x^6}{35x^6}$

1 Decide whether each of the following is an expression, an equation, an identity or a formula.

a $2x = x + x$

b $5x^2 + 3 = 2x$

c $6x^2 - 2x + 5$

d $(x + 2)(x - 3) = 0$

e $2x + 5 = 7x$

f $y = x^2 + 7$

2 Expand

a $x(x^2 + 2x + 5)$

b $x^2(x^2 + 2x + 5)$

c $2x^2(x^2 + 2x + 5)$

d $2x^2(x^2 - 2x)$

3 Factorise each expression fully.

a $3y^2 + 10y$

$y(3y + \quad)$

b $2y^3 + 8y$

> Take the common factor of $2y$ outside a bracket.

c $9y^4 - 6y^2$

4 Factorise each expression completely. Check your answers by expanding.

a $3xy + 9y + 12yz$

b $5x^2 + 10xy + 25xz$

5 Show that $20xy - 8x^2y^2 + 4xz \equiv 4x(5y - 2xy^2 + 4xz)$

Check   Tick each box as your **confidence** in this topic improves.   ☹ 😐 ☺   **Need extra help?** Go to page 50 and tick the boxes next to Q7 and 8. Then try them once you've finished 5.1–5.6.

46

1 Solve these equations.

a $5x - 11 = \dfrac{7x - 1}{3}$

b $\dfrac{5x + 2}{8} = x - 2$

> Clear the fraction by multiplying both sides by the denominator.

2 Problem-solving Hamza and Zikra are thinking of the same number.
Hamza multiplies it by 3, then subtracts 7.
Zikra multiplies it by 11, adds 1, then divides the result by 5.
They both get the same answer. What number did they start with?

3 Solve

a $\dfrac{3x + 7}{2} = \dfrac{x - 7}{3}$

b $\dfrac{5x - 3}{4} = \dfrac{7x + 1}{3}$

c $\dfrac{4x + 3}{5} = \dfrac{7x + 4}{9}$

Guided

$\dfrac{6(3x + 7)}{2} = \dfrac{6(x - 7)}{3}$

> To remove the fractions, multiply both sides of the equation by the LCM of 2 and 3, which is 6.

$\dfrac{3\,6(3x + 7)}{2} = \dfrac{2\,6(x - 7)}{3}$

$3(3x + 7) = 2(x - 7)$

> Cancel the denominators.
> $6 \div 2 = 3$ and $6 \div 3 = 2$

$9x + 21 = 2x - 14$

> Expand the brackets.

$9x - 2x = -14 - 21$

$7x = -35$

> Collect like terms.

$x = -5$

> $-35 \div 7 = -5$

Check:

LHS: $\dfrac{3x + 7}{2} = \dfrac{3(-5) + 7}{2} = \dfrac{-8}{2} = -4$

RHS: $\dfrac{x - 7}{3} = \dfrac{-5 - 7}{3} = \dfrac{-12}{2} = -4$

> Check that the solution is correct by substituting $x = -5$ into both sides of the equation.

4 Problem-solving The diagram shows a regular hexagon.
Work out the perimeter of the hexagon.

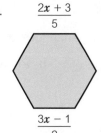

$\dfrac{2x + 3}{5}$

$\dfrac{3x - 1}{2}$

> **Strategy hint**
> Write an equation using the fact that the sides of a regular hexagon are the same length. Solve it to find the value of x. Then work out the side length and perimeter.

Check Tick each box as your **confidence** in this topic improves. ☹ 😐 ☺

Need extra help? Go to page 51 and tick the box next to Q9. Then try it once you've finished 5.1–5.6.

1 Make x the subject of each formula.

a $p = x + 7$ **b** $m = x - 10$ **c** $y = 2x$ **d** $h = \dfrac{x}{3}$

> The **subject** of a formula is the variable on its own on one side of the equals sign. A is the subject of $A = l \times b$.

Guided

2 Make x the subject of each formula.

a $y = 3x + 5$ **b** $z = 8x - 9$ **c** $p = 4x + 3q$

$y - 5 = 3x$

$x = \dfrac{y - 5}{\square}$

> Rearrange the formula so it starts '$x =$'.

3 Make r the subject of each formula.

a $A = \pi r l$ **b** $A = \pi r^2$ **c** $A = \dfrac{\pi r^2}{2}$ **d** $V = \dfrac{\pi r^2 h}{3}$

> $r^2 = \dfrac{A}{\pi}$
> $r = \square$

4 **Problem-solving** The diagram shows a trapezium with area $168\,\text{cm}^2$.

  a Write down the formula for the area of a trapezium. ....

  b Rearrange the formula to make b the subject.

  c Work out the value of b.

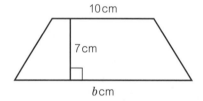

10 cm

7 cm

b cm

5 Make x the subject of each formula.

Guided

  a $px - 5 = qx + r$

    $px - qx = r + 5$ — Get all the terms in x onto one side.

    $x(p - q) = r + 5$ — x is a common factor of both terms, so factorise.

    $x = \dfrac{r + 5}{p - q}$ — Divide both sides by $(p - q)$ to make x the subject.

  b $5x + m = x + 8$ **c** $xz - 9 = 15 + 2x$ **d** $p^2 x = q^2 x + pq$

> The subject of a formula should only appear once in the formula.

6 Make y the subject of each formula.

  a $C = 3W + \sqrt{y}$ **b** $P = K + 2\sqrt{y}$ **c** $A = 5x + \dfrac{\sqrt{3y}}{z}$

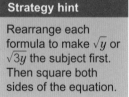

> **Strategy hint**
>
> Rearrange each formula to make $\sqrt{y}$ or $\sqrt{3y}$ the subject first. Then square both sides of the equation.

Check   Tick each box as your **confidence** in this topic improves.   ☹ 😐 ☺   **Need extra help?** Go to page 51 and tick the boxes next to Q10–11. Then try them once you've finished 5.1–5.6.

48

Substitution

□ **1** Work out the value of each expression when $a = 2$, $b = 5$ and $c = -3$.

a $ab = a \times b = 2 \times \ldots = \ldots$

b $ab + c = a \times b + c = 2 \times \ldots + (-3) = \ldots + (-3) = \ldots$

c $(ab)^2 = (a \times b)^2 = (2 \times \ldots)^2 = (\ldots)^2 = \ldots$

d $(a + b)^2 = (\ldots + \ldots)^2 = (\ldots)^2 = \ldots$

e $(a + b)^2 - c = (\ldots + \ldots)^2 - (\ldots) = (\ldots)^2 - (\ldots) = \ldots$

Follow the priority of operations: Brackets, Indices, Multiplication/Division, Addition/Subtraction.

Inequalities

□ **2** Match each of these inequalities with the correct number line diagram.

o shows the value is not included.
● shows the value is included.

a $x \geqslant -3$ **b** $x < 3$ **c** $-3 < x \leqslant 3$ **d** $-3 \leqslant x < 3$ .....

i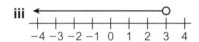

ii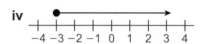

iii

iv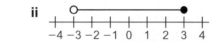

□ **3** Solve these double inequalities. Represent each solution on a number line.

a $5 \leqslant 3x + 2 < 20$ **b** $-2 < x + 1 \leqslant 5$

Worked example

$$5 \leqslant 3x + 2 \qquad 3x + 2 < 20$$
$$5 - 2 \leqslant 3x \qquad 3x < 20 - 2$$
$$3 \leqslant 3x \qquad 3x < 18$$
$$1 \leqslant x \qquad x < 6$$

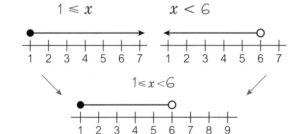

$1 \leqslant x < 6$

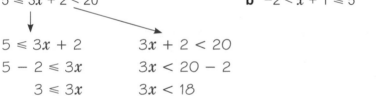

c $4 > \dfrac{x}{2} > -1$ **d** $-3 \leqslant 2x - 1 \leqslant 11$ **e** $-1 \leqslant 3x + 5 < 8$

Rewrite part **c** as $-1 < \dfrac{x}{2} < 4$

□ **4** Solve these inequalities.

a $6 - x \leqslant 1$ **b** $-4a \geqslant -20$ **c** $-14 < 7m < 35$

In part **a**, add x to both sides so it is no longer negative.

Using index laws

5 Work out $5x^0$.

$5x^0 = 5 \times 1 =$ ....

6 Simplify these expressions.

Write each one as **i** a fraction **ii** a negative power.

a $\dfrac{x^2}{x^7}$ **b** $\dfrac{p^3}{p^{10}}$ **c** $\dfrac{q}{q^5}$

i $\dfrac{x^2}{x^7} = \dfrac{x \times x}{x \times x \times x \times x \times x \times x \times x}$

    $= \dfrac{1}{x^{\cdots}}$

ii $\dfrac{1}{x^{\cdots}} = x^{\cdots}$

Expanding and factorising

7 Complete the grids to expand the brackets.

a $a(a^2 + 7a) =$ ..... + ...

a	a^2	$7a$
a	$a \times a^2 =$	$a \times 7a =$ .....

b $b^2(b^2 + 3b - 1) =$ ..... + ... − .....

	b^2	$3b$	-1
b^2	$b^2 \times b^2 =$	$b^2 \times 3b =$	$b^2 \times -1 =$ .....

c $2c(c^2 - 3c + 4) =$ ..... − ..... + ...

	c^2	$-3c$	$+4$
$2c$	$2c \times c^2 =$	$2c \times -3c =$	$3c \times 4 =$ .....

8 Complete to fully factorise these expressions.

a $2y^3 + y = y($ ..... $+ 1)$

b $3y^3 + 2y^2 = y^2($ ..... $+$ ..... $)$

c $5y^2 + 15y = 5y($ ..... $+$ ..... $)$

d $6y^4 + 9y =$ ..... $(2y^3 +$ ..... $)$

e $10y^2 - 15y =$ ..... $(2y -$ ..... $)$

Solving equations

☐ **9** The diagram shows a square.

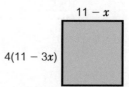

$11 - x$

$4(11 - 3x)$

   a Write an equation involving x.

   b Solve your equation to work out the value of x.

   c Work out the side length of the square.

Changing the subject

☐ **10** Make x the subject of each formula.

Guided

   a $p = x + q$ $x \longrightarrow \boxed{+ q} \longrightarrow p$ **b** $y = 8x$ **c** $y = 7x - t$

       $p = x + q$

       $x = p - q$ $x \longleftarrow \boxed{- q} \longleftarrow q$

   d $A = 5x^2$ $x \longrightarrow \boxed{\square^2} \longrightarrow \boxed{\times 5} \longrightarrow A$ **e** $m = nx^2$

                     $x \longleftarrow \boxed{\sqrt{}} \longleftarrow \boxed{\div 5} \longleftarrow A$

☐ **11** Make x the subject of each formula.

Guided

   a $4x = mx + n$ **b** $ax + b = x + c$

       $4x - mx = n$ | Rearrange to get only the terms in x on the left-hand side of the equation. |

       $x(4 - m) = n$ | Factorise the left-hand side. |

       $x = \dfrac{n}{\square - \square}$

   c $px + 7 = 12 - qx$ **d** $A = \sqrt{\dfrac{x}{9}}$ **e** $E = \dfrac{\sqrt{6x}}{5}$

                            $A^2 = \dfrac{x}{9}$

                            $x = \text{.......} A^2$

1 Simplify

a $\dfrac{14x^9}{4x^{13}}$ ....

b $\dfrac{30x^3}{12x^{10}}$ ....

c $\dfrac{a^3 \times a^5}{a^{11}}$ ....

d $\dfrac{t^8}{t^5 \times t^4}$ ....

e $\dfrac{25b^7}{15b \times b^8}$ ....

In parts **d** and **e** simplify the denominator first.

Guided

2 Solve these inequalities. Write your answer as a mixed number. Represent the solution on a number line.

a $x + 3\frac{1}{5} \leqslant 5\frac{4}{5}$

b $6x > -23$

c $\dfrac{x}{2} < 3\frac{2}{3}$

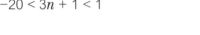

$x \leqslant 5\frac{4}{5} - 3\frac{1}{5}$

3 **Problem-solving** Here are two inequalities.

$-8 \leqslant 5n - 3 < 7 \qquad -20 < 3n + 1 < 1$

n is an integer.

What is the value of n?

Strategy hint

Solve each inequality and represent both solutions on the same number line.

4 **Problem-solving** The isosceles trapezium in the diagram is made up of three equilateral triangles joined together. Work out the value of x.

Write your answer as a mixed number in its simplest form.

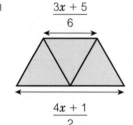

$\dfrac{3x + 5}{6}$

$\dfrac{4x + 1}{2}$

Strategy hint

Set up an equation using $b = 2a$.

5 Write each of these equations in the form $y = mx + c$.

a $2y + 8x = 5$

b $12x - 6y + 7 = 0$

c $8y - 3x - 5 = 0$

Leave any numbers that don't divide exactly as improper fractions or mixed numbers.

6 **STEM / Modelling** A formula used to work out the speed (v) of an object is $v^2 = u^2 + 2as$, where u is the starting speed, a is the acceleration and s is the distance.

a Make s the subject of the formula.

b Work out the value of s when $v = 0$, $u = 20$ and $a = -5$.

Guided

7 Make x the subject of each formula.

a $5x + a = 2(x - 9)$

$5x + a = 2x - 18$

$5x - 2x = $ ....

$3x = $ ....

$x = $ ....

| Expand the brackets. |

| Get all the terms in x onto one side. |

b $p(3x + 4) = 8 - 7x$

c $5(3 + x) = 4q(6x - 9)$

8 The formula $s = \dfrac{(u + v)}{2} t$ is used to calculate the distance travelled by an object moving with constant acceleration, where s = distance, u = initial velocity, v = final velocity and t = time.

A ball is dropped from a window.

a Work out the distance it falls if $u = 0$ m/s, $v = 20$ m/s and $t = 2$ s.

b Another ball is dropped from a height of 80 metres ($s = 80$ m). If $u = 0$ m/s and $v = 40$ m/s, work out how long it takes to fall to the ground.

9 Zainab uses this method to make x the subject of the formula $\dfrac{1}{x} = y - 8$.

$1 = x(y - 8)$ — Multiply both sides by x.

$\dfrac{1}{y - 8} = x$ — Divide both sides by $(y - 8)$.

$x = \dfrac{1}{y - 8}$ — Rewrite with x on the left-hand side.

Use Zainab's method to make x the subject of each of these formulae.

a $\dfrac{1}{x} = y + 5$

b $\dfrac{1}{x} = c - 3$

c $\dfrac{4}{x} = y + 1$

Guided

10 Make x the subject of each formula.

a $\dfrac{1}{x} = \dfrac{1}{t} + \dfrac{1}{u}$

$\dfrac{1}{x} = \dfrac{\square + \square}{tu}$

$tu = x(\text{.......} + \text{.......})$

$x = $ ....

b $\dfrac{1}{x} - \dfrac{3}{a} = \dfrac{5}{b}$

c $\dfrac{7}{x} - \dfrac{3}{v} = \dfrac{2}{y}$

5

Unit test

1 Work out the value of $x^2 - (x+y)^2$ when $x = 5$ and $y = -2$.

2 Work out the value of $6x^0 \times 9y^0$ ....

3 Write $\dfrac{x^7}{x^{12}}$ as a single power of x. ....

4 Solve these inequalities. Show each solution on a number line.

   a $x - 5 > -3$ **b** $5x \geqslant -20$ **c** $-9 \leqslant 2x - 3 < 7$ **d** $4 - x \leqslant -2$

5 Solve the equation $\dfrac{7x + 1}{5} = \dfrac{4x + 2}{3}$

6 Expand

   a $2y^2(10 - y^2)$ ....

   b $x(x^2 + 3x + 4)$ ....

7 Factorise each expression completely. Check your answers by expanding.

   a $14x^3 = 21x^2$ ....

   b $2xy + 6xy^2 + 8xz$ ....

8 Make x the subject of each formula.

   a $y = 7x + 2$

   b $A = tx^2$

   c $ax - 3 = bx + 4$

   d $s = \dfrac{\sqrt{5x}}{t}$

   e $\dfrac{1}{x} = y + z$

1 For the following data:

    i decide whether it is primary or secondary data

    ii if it is primary data, give a suitable method for collecting it.

    a The number of births in the UK from 1 January 2013 to 31 December 2013

    b Flavours chosen by people you asked to name their favourite flavour ice cream

    c The number of people who use the cycle lane on a main road

> **Primary data** is data you collect yourself. **Secondary data** is collected by someone else. Different ways of collecting primary data include questionnaires, surveys and data logging.

2 **Reasoning / STEM** Circle the most appropriate sample size for each survey. Explain your choice.

    a The population of Leeds is 750 000. The council wants to find out how many people have their recommended six-monthly check-up with their dentist.

        75   8000   80 000   700

    10% of 750 000 is 75 000 so appropriate sample size is ....

    b There are 20 000 seeds in a box. Researchers want to find out how many seeds will germinate.

        250   2000   10 000   20

Guided

> The total number of items your survey relates to is called the **population**.
> The group of items you test is called a **sample**. Sampling can be time consuming and expensive but the greater the sample, the more reliable it can be. For a sample to be reliable and unbiased, it should
> - be at least 10% of the population
> - represent the population.

> **Literacy hint**
>
> **Bias** means that results are not equally likely, for example because a sample isn't picked at random or a survey question doesn't include all the possible options.

3 Explain why each of these questions is unsuitable to use in a survey. For each one write a more suitable question to replace it.

    a What methods of transport have you used to travel to school this month?

        Car ☐   Bus ☐   Train ☐   Cycle ☐

    b What do you do after school?

> A question in a survey can be biased if it encourages people to give a particular answer. A good survey question should not be vague, leading or restrictive.

> **Literacy hint**
>
> A **leading question** encourages people to give a particular answer.

4 **Reasoning / Real** A survey is set up to find out the most common second language of people living in London. The sample is all the staff who work at a food chain.

    a What is the population for the survey?

    b Is the sample random? Explain your answer.

> In a **random sample**, the whole population has an equal chance of being chosen, so it reduces the chances of bias.

Check   Tick each box as your **confidence** in this topic improves.   **Need extra help?** Go to page 59 and tick the box next to Q1. Then try it once you've finished 6.1–6.4.

Guided

1 Anti-aircraft campaigners want to find out how people feel about using a plane to go on holiday. They ask, 'It is stupid to fly to a holiday when there are lots of great holidays here in this country, don't you agree?'

   a What do you think most people will answer?   They will *agree*.

   b Why is this a leading question?

   The question implies you're stupid if you don't agree.

> A leading question encourages people to give a particular answer.

   c Rewrite the question to find out what people really think about using a plane to go on holiday.

> Your question should be precise and should not lead to a particular answer.

2 Here are some records from a dentist's database of patients.

   a Design a grouped frequency table to record the patients' ages.

> A grouped frequency table usually has 4 or 5 equal width classes. You can add a tally column for recording the data.

Name	Age	Number of fillings
G. Nasher	23	2
A. Sweet	21	7
C. Risp	59	7
P. Late	39	11
D. Kay	46	11
F. Alsies	56	9
C. Runchie	23	10
B. Race	52	5
D. Rill	56	12
I. N. Jection	60	9
S. Mile	51	3
B. Rush	58	4
C. Rown	63	6
F. Illings	28	6

  b i Complete this two-way table to show the number of fillings and the ages of the patients.

		Number of fillings		
		1–5	6–10	11+
Age, a (years)	$20 \leqslant a \leqslant 39$			
	$40 \leqslant a \leqslant 59$			
	60+			

> A two-way table shows data sorted according to two sets of categories.

   ii How many patients who are less than 40 years old have 6 or more fillings?

   iii What proportion of the patients have between 6 and 10 fillings?

3 Design your own questionnaire to test this hypothesis.

   'Most students in Year 9 sleep at least 10 hours on a school night.'

> Think about what data you want to collect, and how you might collect it.
> Make sure your questions are easily understood and not 'leading'.
> Check that you can record all possible answers given.

Check   Tick each box as your **confidence** in this topic improves.

Need extra help? Go to page 59 and tick the boxes next to Q2–5. Then try them once you've finished 6.1–6.4.

56

1 The table shows the results of a survey into the heights of a group of Year 9 students. Work out an estimate for

a the range

b the mean.

When data has been grouped, you cannot work out the exact mean but you can work out an **estimate**.

Height, H (cm)	Frequency	Midpoint of class (cm)	Midpoint × Frequency
$140 < H \leqslant 150$	3	145	435
$150 < H \leqslant 160$	7	155	1085
$160 < H \leqslant 170$	19		
$170 < H \leqslant 180$	3		
Total	32	Total	

You don't know the exact value of each length, so estimate it as the midpoint of each class. Draw a column for the midpoints.
Calculate an estimate of the total height for each class (midpoint × frequency).

Calculate the total number of students and an estimate for the sum of their heights.

Estimated mean = estimated sum of heights ÷ total number of students

= .... ÷ 32

= .... cm (to 2 d.p.)

Worked example

2 Problem-solving The frequency polygon shows the results of a marathon. Work out an estimate for

a the range

b the mean.

Strategy hint

Make a table with these four columns:
• class
• frequency
• midpoint of class
• midpoint × frequency.

c How many people took part in the marathon? ....

d Which number item is the median? ....

e In which group will the median value be? ....

f What is the modal class? ....

You can't work out the median from grouped data but you can find out which group the median value is in.

Check Tick each box as your **confidence** in this topic improves.

Need extra help? Go to page 60 and tick the box next to Q6. Then try it once you've finished 6.1–6.4.

57

1 Saburo is investigating how much local engineering firms pay their staff. The grouped frequency table shows the yearly earnings of staff at one engineering company.

Earnings, e	Number of employees
$0 < e \le £15\,000$	13
$£15\,000 < e \le £30\,000$	4
$£30\,000 < e \le £45\,000$	8
$£45\,000 < e \le £60\,000$	10

a Draw a frequency polygon for this data.

Earnings at engineering companies

[Frequency polygon graph: x-axis "Earnings (£1000)" from 0 to 60, y-axis "Frequency" from 0 to 12]

First draw a frequency diagram. You can draw a frequency polygon by joining the midpoints of the tops of the bars in a frequency diagram.

Earnings, e	Number of employees
$0 < e \le £15\,000$	3
$£15\,000 < e \le £30\,000$	10
$£30\,000 < e \le £45\,000$	8
$£45\,000 < e \le £60\,000$	4

The second grouped frequency table shows yearly earnings at a different engineering company.

b Construct a frequency polygon for this data on the axes used in part **a**.

c Compare the pay for the two companies.

d How could Saburo investigate further?

Do you need to draw a frequency diagram first or can you simply construct a frequency polygon?

Worked example

2 The manager of a shoe shop records the number of customers and the number of sales per day for two weeks. She draws this graph.

a What type of correlation does the graph show? ....

b Draw a line of best fit.

c Circle an outlier and suggest what might have caused it.

An outlier is a value that doesn't follow the trend.

Number of sales against number of customers

[Scatter graph: x-axis "Number of customers" from 0 to 120, y-axis "Number of sales" from 0 to 70]

d Use the line of best fit to estimate the number of sales when 65 customers visit. ....

Find 65 on the correct axis. Draw a line up to the line of best fit and then across to the other axis.

e Use the line of best fit to estimate the number of customers who visited when 50 sales are made.

The manager says, 'About half of all customers buy something.'

f Does the data collected support this statement? ....

g Explain what you would need to do to investigate this statement further.

Check Tick each box as your **confidence** in this topic improves. ☹ 😐 ☺

Need extra help? Go to page 60 and tick the boxes next to Q7 and 8. Then try them once you've finished 6.1–6.4.

Planning a survey

☐ **1** Gina is doing a social studies investigation on TV viewing.

> I collect primary data for my investigation.
> Someone else collects secondary data.

    a She asks 25 people at random in her street.
    Is this primary or secondary data?

    b She looks on the internet for UK viewing figures. Is this primary or secondary data?

Collecting data

☐ **2** A researcher measures the lengths of a sample of 100 daffodil leaves using a ruler.

    a What level of accuracy should the lengths be measured to? ....

    A the nearest millimetre   **B** the nearest centimetre   **C** the nearest metre

    b The researcher suggests putting the lengths into the following groups.

    0–10 cm   10–20 cm   20–30 cm

    In which groups could she record a 20 cm long leaf? ....

    c What is the problem with her choice of groups? ....
    She redesigns her groups.

    d Complete the new groups.   0–9 cm   10–..........cm   20–..........cm

☐ **3** For each place, suggest a suitable sample size for surveying
the number of people who use public libraries.

    a Huntly (population 8055)

    b Townsville (population 171 380)

    c Singapore (population 2 553 379)

☐ **4** Would you use primary or secondary data to investigate each of these?

> If you obtain the
> data yourself, then
> it is primary data.

    a How much pocket money students at your school get per week ....

    b The number of road traffic accidents in Birmingham ....

    c How many people in your area eat their five-a-day fruit and vegetables ....

☐ **5** **Reasoning** A research company wants to find out how often people exercise.
Explain how each sample is biased.

> People leaving a swimming
> pool don't represent the
> whole population because ...

    a Only people leaving a swimming pool.

    b Only people on a football team.

    c Only students at a school.

Calculating averages and range

6 **Real** The table shows the heights of some mountains around the world.

Height, H (metres)	Frequency
$4000 < H \leqslant 5000$	8
$5000 < H \leqslant 6000$	4
$6000 < H \leqslant 7000$	3
$7000 < H \leqslant 8000$	2
$8000 < H \leqslant 9000$	2

a How high could the tallest of these mountains be? ....

b How high could the least tall of these mountains be? ....

c Use your answers to parts **a** and **b** to estimate the range. ....

d How many mountains were surveyed? ....

e The midpoint of $4000 < H \leqslant 5000$ is 4500.
Work out the midpoints for the other groups and write them in a new column in the table.

f Work out midpoint × frequency for each row and write them in a new column in the table.

g Use your answers to parts **d** and **f** to estimate the mean.

Displaying and analysing data

7 Gedi recorded the lengths of some of his runner beans.

Length, l (cm)	Midpoint	Frequency
$10 \leqslant l < 15$	12.5	5
$15 \leqslant l < 20$		25
$20 \leqslant l < 25$		20

a Complete the table.

b Draw a frequency polygon for this data.

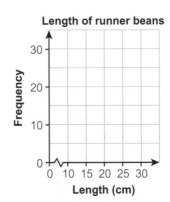
Length of runner beans

8 The scatter graph show the relationship between the maximum daily temperature and the number of visitors to a zoo.

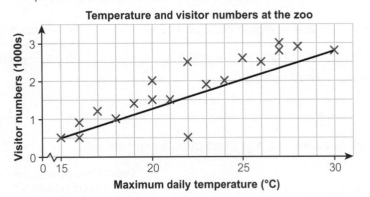

a What type of correlation does the graph show? ....

b Put a ring around the outlier.

c The line of best fit is not accurate.
What has been done incorrectly?

d Draw a line of best fit.

e Predict the number of visitors when the maximum daily temperature is 22°C.
....

f Predict the maximum daily temperature when the number of visitors is 2000.
....

Literacy hint

Outliers are data points that don't follow the trend.

Worked example

1 The table shows the results of an IQ test taken by a group of students.

Test result	Frequency
60–79	8
80–99	48
100–119	83
120–139	11

a Work out an estimate for the mean IQ result.

b Which class contains the median IQ?

2 **STEM** A veterinary nurse records the age and mass of some kittens.

Age (days)	14	22	21	18	34	25	40	37	41	37	24	20
Mass (g)	170	250	240	220	270	280	390	360	400	380	270	240

a Plot a scatter diagram for this information. Give a title and label the axes.

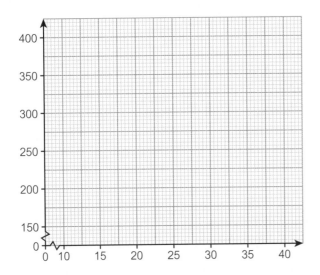

Worked example

b Put a ring around the data point that is an outlier.
What might be the cause of this outlier?

c Draw a line of best fit on the scatter diagram. Use it to estimate

i the mass of a kitten that is 30 days old ....

ii the age of a kitten with a mass of 150 g. ....

d How reliable do you think your answer to part **c ii** is? Explain your answer.

3 Real The tables show the population (in millions) of the UK in 2010 and the projected UK population in 2035.

2010

Age, a (years)	Male	Female
$0 \leqslant a < 20$	7.6	7.2
$20 \leqslant a < 40$	8.4	8.2
$40 \leqslant a < 60$	8.3	8.5
$60 \leqslant a < 80$	5.3	5.9
$80 \leqslant a < 100$	1.1	1.8

2035

Age, a (years)	Male	Female
$0 \leqslant a < 20$	8.4	8.0
$20 \leqslant a < 40$	9.3	8.9
$40 \leqslant a < 60$	9.0	8.7
$60 \leqslant a < 80$	7.2	7.8
$80 \leqslant a < 100$	2.5	3.3

a Write down the modal age group for

   i 2010 ....

   ii 2035. ....

b Calculate an estimate of the mean for

   i 2010 ....

   ii 2035. ....

c Write three sentences comparing the populations of the UK in 2010 and 2035.

4 Reasoning / Real The table shows the times, in minutes and seconds, of two 5000 m races.

Time, T	Frequency	
	Race 1	Race 2
13 min 15 s $< T \leqslant$ 13 min 20 s	0	8
13 min 20 s $< T \leqslant$ 13 min 30 s	5	14
13 min 30 s $< T \leqslant$ 13 min 50 s	22	12
13 min 50 s $< T \leqslant$ 14 min 50 s	19	8
14 min 50 s $< T \leqslant$ 15 min 50 s	7	0

a Draw a frequency polygon for the Race 1 data.

b Draw a frequency polygon for the Race 2 data.

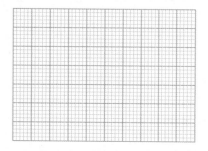
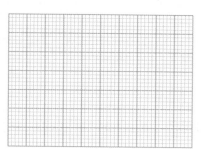

c Write a sentence comparing the times of the 5000 m heats in Race 1 and in Race 2.

1 A headteacher wants to find out her students' views on the new PE facilities.
The school has 2300 students. Circle the most appropriate sample size for the survey.

2300   1000   250   23

2 You are going to investigate this hypothesis. 'Drawing pins always land point up.'
How many times should you drop a drawing pin?   ☐ 10 times   ☐ 100 times   ☐ 1000 times

3 A survey asks
How many films have you watched in the last week?   ☐ 0–3   ☐ 3–6   ☐ 6–9   ☐ 9+

   a Explain what is wrong with the question. ....

   b Rewrite the question. ....

4 Selina says, 'In my village, boys can balance on one leg better than girls.'

   a What data should Selina collect to test her hypothesis?

   b There are 800 students at Selina's school. What sample size should she use?

   c If she timed 20 students standing on one leg, has she found secondary data? Explain.

   d Design a frequency table to record her data.

5 The scatter graph shows the height and mass of
   some professional footballers.

   a What type of correlation does the
      graph show? ....

   b Ring any outliers.

   c Draw a line of best fit.

   d Use your line of best fit to estimate the mass of a
      1.7 m tall footballer. ....

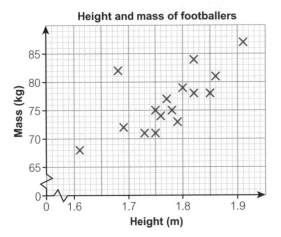

Height and mass of footballers

6 Samir and Maier record
the number of cars
passing their houses
every hour for a day.

Samir's data

Number of cars, n	Frequency
$0 \leq n < 100$	12
$100 \leq n < 200$	10
$200 \leq n < 300$	2

Maier's data

Number of cars, n	Frequency
$0 \leq n < 100$	4
$100 \leq n < 200$	10
$200 \leq n < 300$	8

   a Which is the modal class for

      i Samir's data ....   ii Maier's data? ....

   b Calculate an estimate of the mean for

      i Samir's data ....   ii Maier's data. ....

   c Write a sentence comparing the two sets of data.

1 Real Two friends compare the cost of printing some photographs.
Hana's bill is $16.50 for 150 photographs.
Freya's bill is $9.60 for 80 photographs.
Who has the better deal?

> The cost of printing is in **direct proportion** to the number of photographs.

2 STEM A scientist takes these readings for variables x and y in an experiment.

x	1.3	2.4	2.6
y	10.4	19.2	20.8

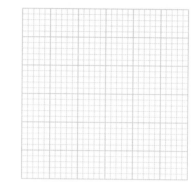

a Plot the points for x and y.

b Does the graph show that the variables are in direct proportion?

c Work out $\frac{y}{x}$ for each pair. What do you notice?

Guided

d Complete the arrow diagram.

e Write a formula linking x and y.

$y = $ x

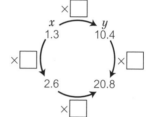

> When two quantities x and y are in direct proportion $\frac{y}{x}$ is constant.

3 Real Grace records the temperature of five cities in August 2014 in Celsius (°C) and in Fahrenheit (°F).

City	Temperature C (°C)	Temperature F (°F)
Athens	33	91
Auckland	17	63
Edinburgh	20	68
Reykjavik	13	55
Stockholm	25	77

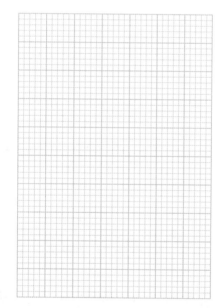

a Is the temperature in Fahrenheit proportional to the temperature in Celsius? Explain.

> Work out $F \div C$ for each city.

b Check your answer to part **a** by drawing a graph, with °C on the horizontal axis.

4 Real The table shows the distances jumped in a long jump final.
Calculate the missing distances a, b and c.
Show your calculations.

Distance (inches)	251.2	328.4	a	332.4	c
Distance (cm)	628	821	814	b	633

> Are centimetres and inches in direct proportion?

Check Tick each box as your **confidence** in this topic improves. ☹ 😐 ☺

Need extra help? Go to page 69 and tick the boxes next to Q1–3. Then try them once you've finished 7.1–7.5.

1 Real / Finance Write a formula linking each pair of quantities.

a The cost, C, in pence of having p photos printed, at 20p per photo.

$$C = \square p$$

b The cost, C, in pounds of b boxes of chocolates at \$3 per box.

c The yearly salary, S, in pounds of a teacher who earns \$$t$ per month.

d The number of miles, m, travelled in 4.5 hours at a speed of h miles per hour.

> **When**
> - y varies as x
> - y varies directly as x
> - y is in direct proportion to x
>
> you can write $y \propto x$
> $y \propto x$ means 'y is proportional to x'.
> When $y \propto x$, then $y = kx$, where k is the **constant of proportionality.**

> **Literacy hint**
>
> In the formula $C = 20p$, 20 is the constant of proportionality. Its value is constant (stays the same) when p and C vary.

2 The price of petrol, P, varies in direct proportion to the amount, a, sold.
The price of 25 litres of petrol is \$30.50.

a Write a formula linking P and a.

$P \propto a$ —— Write the relationship in the form $y \propto x$ and then write the equation in the form $y = kx$.

$P = ka$

When $a = 25$, $P = 30.50$

$30.50 = k \times 25$ —— Substitute the values for P and a into $P = ka$.

$k = \dfrac{30.50}{25} = \ldots\ldots\ldots$ —— Solve the equation to find k. Rewrite the equation using the value of k.

$P = \ldots\ldots\ldots a$

b Use your formula to work out the price of 40 litres of petrol.

3 Finance The Australian dollar, A, varies in direct proportion with the UK pound, P.
One day 117 Australian dollars = £65.

a Write a formula for converting pounds to Australian dollars. Write a formula $A = \square$

> **Worked example**

b How many Australian dollars can you buy with £150?

c How many UK pounds can you buy with 500 Australian dollars?
Round your answer to an appropriate level of accuracy.

Check Tick each box as your **confidence** in this topic improves.

Need extra help? Go to page 69 and tick the boxes next to Q4–5. Then try them once you've finished 7.1–7.5.

Translations and enlargements

1 a Translate shape A by the column vector $\begin{pmatrix} 8 \\ -2 \end{pmatrix}$.
Label the image B.

b Write down the column vector that maps shape C onto shape A.

> In a column vector, the top number represents the movement to the right or left. The bottom number represents the movement up or down.

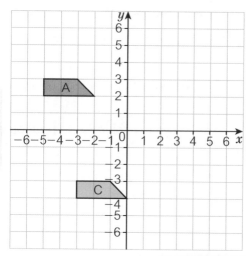

2 Enlarge these shapes by scale factor 2.
Use the marked centre of enlargement.

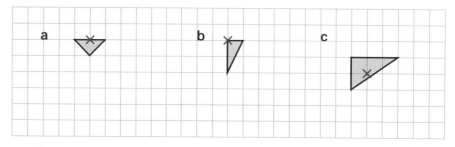

> **Worked example**

3 Describe the enlargement that takes shape A to shape B in each of these diagrams.

a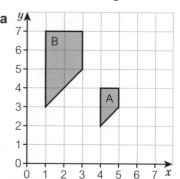

b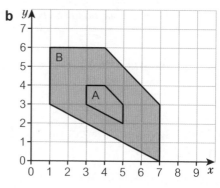

> To describe an enlargement, give the scale factor and the coordinates of the centre of enlargement.

> When you enlarge a shape by a scale factor from a centre of enlargement, the distance from the centre to each point on the shape is also multiplied by the scale factor.

4 a Enlarge triangle A by scale factor 2, centre of enlargement (0, 0). Label the image B.

b Enlarge triangle A by scale factor 2, centre of enlargement (6, 1). Label the image C.

c Enlarge triangle A by scale factor 3, centre of enlargement (2, 3). Label the image D.

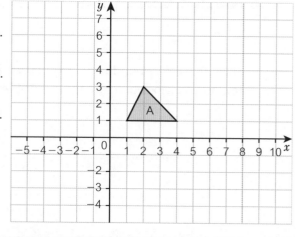

Check Tick each box as your **confidence** in this topic improves.

Need extra help? Go to page 70 and tick the box next to Q6. Then try it once you've finished 7.1–7.5.

1 Enlarge the shape using the same marked centre of enlargement and the negative scale factors shown.

> A negative scale factor has the same effect as a positive scale factor except that it takes the image to the opposite side of the centre of enlargement.

a Scale factor −2

b Scale factor −4

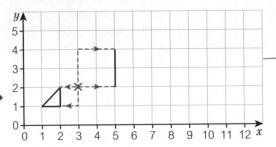

> Count the squares from the centre of enlargement.
> For scale factor of −2
> • the top vertex of the small triangle changes to the bottom vertex of the enlarged triangle, from 1 left to 2 right
> • the bottom right vertex of the triangle changes to the top left vertex of the enlarged triangle, from 1 down and 1 left to 2 up and 2 right.

Guided

2 Enlarge the shapes using the marked centres of enlargement and fractional scale factors.

a scale factor $\frac{1}{2}$

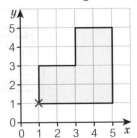

> **Literacy hint**
> You still use the word 'enlarge' for fractional scale factors, even though they make the shape smaller.

b scale factor $\frac{1}{3}$

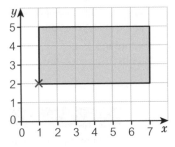

> You can enlarge a shape using a fractional scale factor. Use the same method of multiplying the length of each side by the scale factor.

3 **a** Enlarge shape A using scale factor $\frac{1}{2}$ and centre of enlargement (7, 0). Label the shape B.

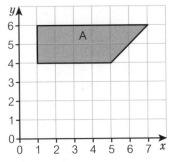

b Write the ratio of the lengths of the sides of shape A to shape B.

c Write the enlargement that will take shape B back to shape A.

> Remember to include the scale factor and the centre of enlargement.

Check Tick each box as your **confidence** in this topic improves.

Need extra help? Go to page 70 and tick the box next to Q6. Then try it once you've finished 7.1–7.5.

Guided

1 Finance In one year the value of Anup's investments dropped by 5% to $6175.

How much were Anup's investments worth at the start of the year?

100% − 5% = 95% = 0.95

Original number → ×0.95 → 6175 ── | Draw a function machine. |

> You can use inverse operations to find the original amount after a percentage increase or decrease.

.... ← ÷0.95 ← 6175

Anup's investments were worth .... at the start of the year.

2 Finance / Problem-solving Dai bought a pair of trainers for $52.
They had been reduced by 20%.

a What was the original price of the trainers before the reduction?

Hammi bought a pair of trainers for $28. They had been reduced by 30%.

b Who saved more money?

> **Worked example**

3 Finance Wamil invests $2500. A year later the investment is worth $2650.

Work out the percentage increase in her investment.

 Guided

Actual change = $2650 − $2500 = $..............

$$\text{Percentage change} = \frac{\text{actual change}}{\text{original amount}} \times 100$$

$$= \frac{......}{2500} \times 100 = ...\%$$

> You can calculate a percentage change using the formula
> $$\text{percentage change} = \frac{\text{actual change}}{\text{original amount}} \times 100$$

4 Finance Jin invests $7000.
When her investment matures she receives $8540.

Work out the percentage increase in her investment.

> **Literacy hint**
> An investment 'matures' when the investment period (e.g. 5 years) ends.

5 Finance / Real The cost of the London 2012 Olympic and Paralympic Games decreased from an estimated £9.30 billion to a final cost of £8.92 billion.
What was the percentage decrease in the estimated cost?
Give your answer to the nearest whole number.

> You don't need to write the billions.
> 9.30 − 8.92 = ☐

Check Tick each box as your **confidence** in this topic improves.

Need extra help? Go to page 70 and tick the boxes next to Q7 and 8. Then try them once you've finished 7.1–7.5.

Direct proportion

1 P and Q are in direct proportion.
Find the missing values a and b
in this table.

P	Q
4	9
12	a
b	72

Use equivalent ratios.

$$\times\square \begin{array}{c} P : Q \\ 4 : 9 \\ 12 : a \end{array} \times\square \qquad \times\square \begin{array}{c} P : Q \\ 4 : 9 \\ b : 72 \end{array} \times\square$$

2 A mechanic charges \$78 for 3 hours' work and \$208 for 8 hours' work.
Are his charges in direct proportion to the length of time worked?

£78

| 1 hour | 1 hour | 1 hour |

How much for 1 hour?
Multiply it by 8.
Does this equal \$208?

3 Finance The Indian rupee, R, varies in direct proportion
with the UK pound, P. One day, £80 is worth 7760 rupees.

Substitute $P = 130$
into your formula.

   a How many Indian rupees can you buy with £1?

   b Write the formula relating the Indian rupee, R, to the UK pound, P.
     $R = \ldots\ldots\ldots\ldots P$

   c How many Indian rupees can you buy with £130?

Solving problems using direct proportion

4 P is directly proportional to Q.

$\propto$ means 'is proportional
to' so $y \propto x$ is another
way of saying $y = kx$.

   a Write this as a formula using algebra.

   $P \propto \ldots\ldots\ldots$

   $P = k \ldots\ldots\ldots$

   When $P = 23.4$, $Q = 6.5$.

   b Substitute the values into your '$P = k\,\square$' formula from part **a**. $\ldots\ldots\ldots$

   c Solve to find k.

   d Rewrite the formula as $P = \square\,Q$. $\ldots\ldots\ldots$

   e Use your formula from part **d** to find the value of P when $Q = 15$.

5 a is proportional to the square of b. When $a = 9$, $b = 5$.

$a \propto b^2$
$a = \square\square$

   a Write a formula connecting a and b.

   b Work out the value of a when $b = 11$.

Translations and enlargements

6 Look at the coordinate grid.

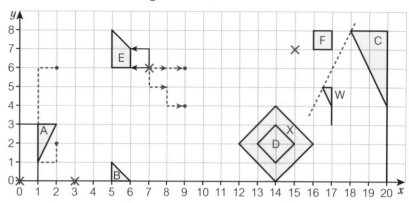

a Enlarge shape A with a scale factor 2 from the centre of enlargement (0, 0). Label your image U.

b Enlarge shape B with a scale factor 3 from the centre of enlargement (3, 0). Label your image V.

> Draw an arrow from the centre to a vertex. Multiply the arrow length by the scale factor. Repeat for other vertices.

c Shape C has been enlarged to shape W.
Write down the scale factor and the coordinates of the centre of enlargement. ....

d Shape D has been enlarged to shape X.
Write down the scale factor and the coordinates of the centre of enlargement. ....

> Join the corresponding corners of the shapes with straight lines (the first one has been done for you). Make sure the lines are long enough to cross each other.

e Enlarge shape E with a scale factor −2 from the centre of enlargement (7, 6). Label your image Y.

f Enlarge shape F with a scale factor −2 from the centre of enlargement (15, 7). Label your image Z.

> Draw an arrow from the centre to a vertex. Multiply the arrow length by the scale factor. Draw arrows to the new vertex in the opposite direction. Repeat for other vertices.

Percentage change

7 Work out the original number of members in each of these clubs.

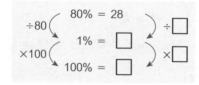

a Decrease of 20%, down to 28 members

28 ÷ 80 × 100 = ...

b Decrease of 40%, down to 72 members

c Increase of 35%, up to 108 members

8 Zafir invests $5000. When his investment matures he receives $5150.

a Complete the working to calculate his percentage increase.
original amount = $5000   actual change = $5150 − $5000 = $150

$$\text{percentage change} = \frac{\text{actual change}}{\text{original amount}} \times 100$$

$$= \frac{\cdots}{\cdots} \times 100 = \ldots\ldots\% $$

> Draw this information as a bar model.
> $5000 $☐
> $5150

b Check your answer by increasing $5000 by the percentage you calculated. Do you get $5150?

1 a Translate shape A by the column
vector $\begin{pmatrix} -6 \\ 2 \end{pmatrix}$. Label the image B.

b Write down the column vector that
maps shape C onto shape B.

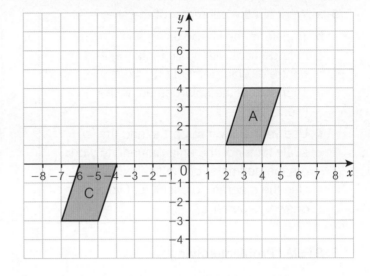

2 Give the scale factor and the centre of
enlargement which takes shape A to
shape B in these diagrams.

a

b

**Worked
example**

3 **Problem-solving** The perimeter of the grey square is 10% greater
than the perimeter of the white square.
Work out the side length of the white square.

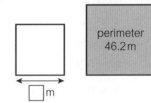

perimeter
46.2 m

☐ m

4 **Problem-solving** Between 2011 and 2012 the earnings of a salesman
increased by 10%. Between 2012 and 2013 his earnings fell 15%.
In 2013 he earned $21 131. How much did he earn in 2011?

Strategy hint

Work out how much he
earned in 2012 first.

5 a Work out the perimeter of the shape.

b Transform the shape using an enlargement with scale factor $-\frac{1}{2}$ and centre of enlargement (12, 4). Then reflect the enlargement in the line $x = 9$.

c Use your answer to part **a**, and the scale factor of the enlargement, to work out the perimeter of the final shape. Use the diagram to check that your answer is correct.

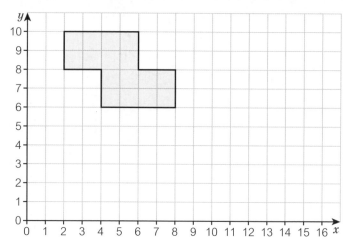

6 STEM / Problem-solving

a Transform the shape using a rotation of 180° about (10, 4), then enlarge it by scale factor −2 using the centre of enlargement at (13, 5).

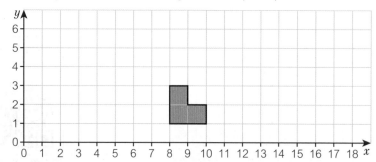

Work out the scale factor.
To find the centre of enlargement use straight lines to join together corresponding corners of the two shapes. Extend these lines across the whole grid. These lines are called rays.

b Describe the single enlargement that will take the finishing shape back to the starting shape.

7 p is proportional to the square of q.
When $p = 8$, $q = 25$.

a What is the value of p when $q = 40$?

b What is the value of q when $p = 12$?

q will have two possible values.

8 Finance The interest, I, earned on a savings account is directly proportional to the amount of money saved, S, and the time, t, the money is saved for, in years. When $6000 is invested for 4 years, the interest earned is $720.

a Work out the value of k, the constant of proportionality.

Work out the interest earned when $4000 is invested for

b 9 years

c 6 months.

1 For each statement

   i are the two quantities in direct proportion?

   ii write a formula to model the situation.

  a The cost, C, in cents of b chocolate bars at 62c each.

  b The phone bill, P, for phone calls at 5c per minute and a $12.95 line rental charge.

2 The values of s and t are in direct proportion. Work out the values of x and y.

s	12	x	27
t	60	95	y

3 a Enlarge shape A using the centre of enlargement (2, 3) and a scale factor 2.

  b Describe the enlargement from shape B to your answer to part **a**.

  c Enlarge shape B using the centre of enlargement (9, 3) with a scale factor −2.

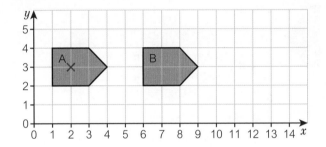

4 a Translate shape P by the column vector $\begin{pmatrix} -5 \\ -2 \end{pmatrix}$. Label it Q.

  b Translate shape Q by the column vector $\begin{pmatrix} 7 \\ -4 \end{pmatrix}$. Label it R.

  c Write down the column vector of the translation that maps shape P onto shape R.

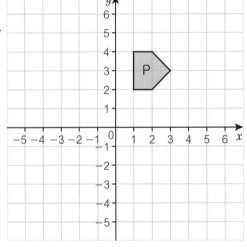

 5 c is proportional to d. When $c = 5.5$, $d = 4$.

  a Write a formula connecting c and d.

  b What is the value of c when $d = 60$?

  c What is the value of d when $c = 33$?

6 In one year the number of members in a table tennis club increased by 20%.
At the end of the year there were 24 members. How many were there at the start of the year?

7 Sachin bought a car for $14 000. He sold it for $5600. Work out his percentage loss.

Maps and scales

1 This diagram shows the plan of a village hall.
1 cm represents 4 m.
Label the real-life lengths in metres.

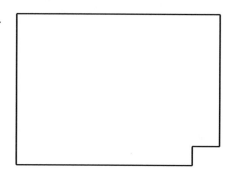

2 On a map, 1 cm represents 150 m.
Work out the real-life distance of

Guided

a 4 cm

Map   Real life
$\times 4 \left(\begin{array}{l} 1\,cm = 150\,m \\ 4\,cm = ...\,m \end{array} \right) \times 4$

b 12 cm

c 25 cm

3 On a map, 1 mm represents 25 m.
Work out the lengths on the map for these real-life distances.

a 500 m ....

b 2000 m ....

c 7 km ....

4 **Real / Problem-solving** Here is a map of Scotland.

a Complete:

.... cm on the map is .... km in real life.

b Estimate the distance in km between

i Glasgow and Edinburgh

ii Inverness and Dundee

iii Perth and Stirling.

Check Tick each box as your **confidence** in this topic improves. ☹ 😐 ☺

Need extra help? Go to page 79 and tick the boxes next to Q1 and 2. Then try them once you've finished 8.1–8.5.

1 Real

a Measure the bearing of Dundee from Inverness.

b Measure the bearing of Inverness from Dundee.

A bearing is an angle in degrees, clockwise from north. A bearing is always written using three digits. This bearing is 025°.

2 Real Draw these bearings accurately. Use the scale 1 cm to 50 km.

Guided

a Gatwick airport is 220 km from Birmingham airport on a bearing of 138°.

$$\times 4.4 \left(\begin{array}{l} 1\,cm = 50\,km \\ 4.4\,cm = 220\,cm \end{array} \right) \times 4.4$$

N

Start from Birmingham airport. Draw the north line.

Draw 138° accurately.

Extend the line to 4.4 cm. Mark Gatwick airport.

Birmingham Airport

Worked example

b East Midlands airport is 136 km from Luton airport on a bearing of 326°.

3

a The bearing of B from A is 100°.
Work out the bearing of A from B.

b The bearing of C from D is 220°.
Work out the bearing of D from C.

c The bearing of E from F is 330°.
Work out the bearing of F from E.

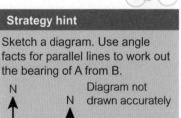

Strategy hint

Sketch a diagram. Use angle facts for parallel lines to work out the bearing of A from B.

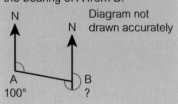

Diagram not drawn accurately

Check Tick each box as your **confidence** in this topic improves.

☹ 😐 ☺

Need extra help? Go to pages 79 and 80 and tick the boxes next to Q4–7. Then try them once you've finished 8.1–8.5.

75

Guided

1 A map has a scale of 1 : 50 000.
What are these distances in real life? Write your answers in metres.

> The scale on a map is given as a ratio 1 : n. For example, 1 : 50 000 means 1 cm on the map represents 50 000 cm in real life.

a 5 cm

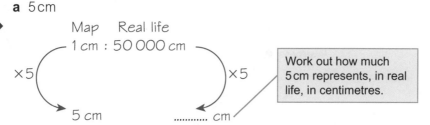

Map   Real life
1 cm : 50 000 cm

×5   ×5

5 cm   .... cm

> Work out how much 5 cm represents, in real life, in centimetres.

1 cm represents 50 000 cm, so 5 cm represents 5 × 50 000 = ... cm

.... cm ÷ 100 = ... m

> Convert the distance to metres.

b 7 cm   **c** 1.5 cm

2 Problem-solving Match the scales **A** to **D** with **i** to **iv**.

   A 1 : 25 000   **B** 1 : 500 000   **C** 1 : 250 000   **D** 1 : 50 000

   i 1 cm to 5 km   **ii** 1 cm to 2.5 km   **iii** 1 cm to 500 m   **iv** 1 cm to 250 m

3 Problem-solving Write each scale as a map ratio.

a 1 cm to 1 km ....   **b** 2 cm to 10 km ....

c 4 cm to 1 km ....   **d** 5 cm to 40 km ....

1 : n

same   units

4 Problem-solving Here is a rough sketch of Phil's garden.

   a Make an accurate scale drawing using a scale of 1 : 200.

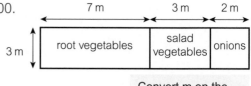

	7 m	3 m	2 m
3 m	root vegetables	salad vegetables	onions

> Convert m on the rough sketch to cm.

   b Next year Phil wants to grow peas. To do this he needs an area of 10 m². Divide the 'root vegetables' patch into two patches, one with an area of 10 m².

   c What area is left for root vegetables next year? ....

5 a What real-life distance does 5 cm represent on maps with these scales?

   i 1 : 10 000   **ii** 1 : 50 000   **iii** 1 : 250 000

   b For each scale, work out the length on the map that represents a real-life distance of 20 km.

   i 1 : 10 000   **ii** 1 : 50 000   **iii** 1 : 250 000

Check   Tick each box as your **confidence** in this topic improves.   ☹ 😐 ☺   **Need extra help?** Go to page 79 and tick the box next to Q3. Then try it once you've finished 8.1–8.5.

Guided

1 Each pair of triangles is congruent. Explain why.

a

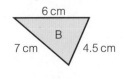

All three sides on triangle A are the same as the sides on triangle B (SSS).

Choose reasons from SSS, SAS, ASA or AAS.

b

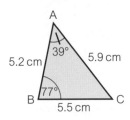

Triangles are congruent if they have equivalent
- SSS (all three sides)
- SAS (two sides and the included angle)
- ASA (two angles and the included side)
- AAS (two angles and another side).

Triangles where all the angles are the same (AAA) are similar, but might not be congruent.

2 Reasoning Circle the triangles that are congruent to triangle ABC. Give reasons.

You may need to work out missing angles.

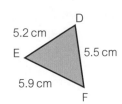
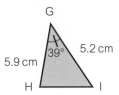
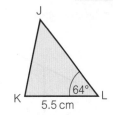

3 Reasoning Explain why triangle ABC is similar to triangle PQR.

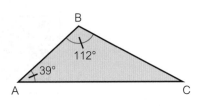
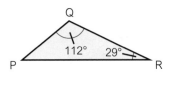

To show that two shapes are similar, show that corresponding angles are equal, or find the scale factor for corresponding sides.

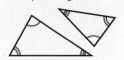

4 Triangle A and triangle B are similar.

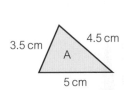
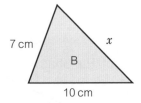

What is the scale factor of the enlargement from A to B?

Work out the missing length in triangle B.

5 These three triangles are similar.
Calculate the lengths labelled with letters.

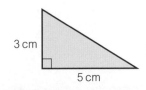
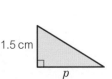
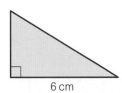

Check Tick each box as your **confidence** in this topic improves. ☹ 😐 ☺

Need extra help? Go to page 80 and tick the boxes next to Q8–10. Then try them once you've finished 8.1–8.5.

77

1 Reasoning

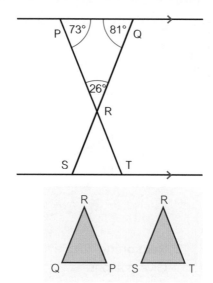

a Find the angles in triangle RST.
Give reasons.

b Are triangles PQR and RST similar? Explain.

c Sketch the triangles the same way up.
Label the vertices and angles.

2 Reasoning

a Explain why triangles ABE and ACD are similar triangles.

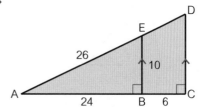

Triangle ABE		Triangle ACD
∠ A	=	∠ A
∠ B = 90°		∠ C = 90°
∠ E	=	∠ D (corresponding angles)

The triangles have the same angles (AAA).

b Calculate the length CD.

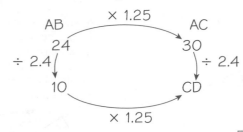

CD = 10 × 1.25 = ...

Worked example

10 × 1.25 is easier to work out than 30 ÷ 2.4, but they both give the same answer.

c Calculate the length DE.

Find the length AD first.

3 Real / Problem-solving Calculate the height of The Shard (a London skyscraper) using similar triangles.

Use the method from Q2.

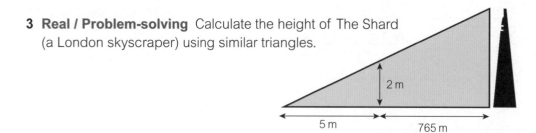

2 m

5 m   765 m

Check Tick each box as your **confidence** in this topic improves.

☹ 😐 ☺

Need extra help? Go to page 80 and tick the box next to Q11. Then try it once you've finished 8.1–8.5.

78

Maps and scales

1 A map has scale 1 cm to 200 m.
What distance on the map represents a real-life length of

    a 400 m ....

    b 100 m ....

    c 500 m ....

    d 1000 m ....

    e 1 km? ....

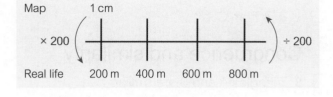

2 A diagram has scale 1 cm to 50 cm.
Calculate the real-life length of

    a 4 cm ....

    b 5 cm ....

    c 10 cm ....

    d 17 cm ....

    e 26 cm ....

3 Write each scale as a ratio.

    a 1 cm to 10 cm = 1 : 10

    b 1 cm to 2 m ....

    c 1 cm to 10 m ....

    d 1 cm to 2 km ....

> In a ratio, both numbers must be in the same units. Convert m and km to cm.

Worked example

Guided

Bearings

4 Write the bearing of B from A in each of these diagrams.

    a   **b**   **c** 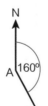   **d**

> A bearing is measured clockwise from north. It is always written as 3 digits. A 37° bearing is written as 037°.

5 Draw an accurate bearing of 065° from the point X.

        X ●

6 Draw an accurate bearing of 310° from the point Y.

        ● Y

7 Measure and write down the bearing of

A ●

    a B from A ....

    b B from C ....

    c C from B ....

    d A from C ....

● B

●
C

Congruence and similarity

8 Triangles A and B are similar.

    a Complete the table showing the pairs of corresponding sides.

    b Use a pair of corresponding sides to work out the scale factor from A to B.

       $3 \times SF = 9$, so SF is ....

    c Use the scale factor to work out x and y.

A	B
3	9
	x
5	

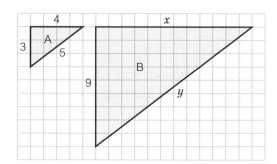

A × scale factor = B
$4 \times \square = x$

Guided

9 Reasoning Find the missing lengths in these similar shapes.

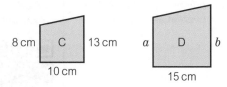

Strategy hint

Draw a table for C and D like the one in Q8.

10 Which of these triangles are similar to triangle A? ....

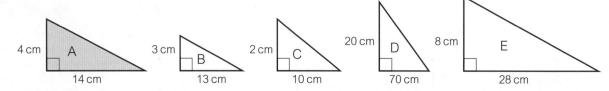

11 Reasoning

    a What can you say about WX and YZ? Explain how you know.

    b Why does angle VWX = angle WYZ?

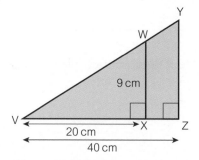

    c What is the scale factor of the enlargement from triangle VWX to VYZ? ....

    d Work out the length YZ.

1 Use a scale of 1 cm : 1 km to draw each bearing accurately.

   a Newtown is 5 km from Treville on a bearing of 070°.

   b Marville is 7 km from Treville on a bearing of 280°.

   c What is the actual distance between Newtown and Marville? ....

Start with Treville.

Worked example

2 Write each map scale as a ratio.

   1 : ☐

   a 2 cm to 1 m ....

   b 4 cm to 1 km ....

   c 8 cm to 5 km ....

3 **Reasoning** In this arrowhead, angle BAD = 30°, angle ABD = 45°.
Calculate

   a angle BDA ....

   b angle BDC ....

   c angle DCB ....

   d Explain why triangles ABD and BCD are congruent.

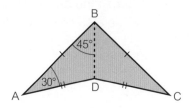

4 **Reasoning** These triangles are all congruent.
Work out the missing sides and angles.

Sketch them all facing
the same way.
For example, like this.

   a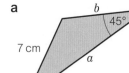

   b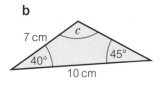

   c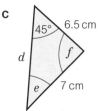

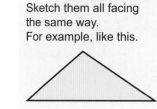

5 **Reasoning**

   a Find the length PR.

   b Find the length PT.

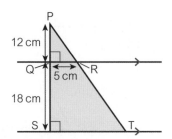

You can use Pythagoras' theorem
to find the lengths of sides in a
right-angled triangle.

6 **Real / Problem-solving** This map shows
some airports in New Zealand.
A plane leaves Nelson airport and travels for
260 km on a bearing of 190°.
It then travels for 750 km on a bearing of 015°.
At which airport does it land?

7 Three phone masts are at the vertices
of an equilateral triangle with side 10 km.
Each has a range of 5 km.

a Draw a scale diagram to show the
areas the phone signal can reach.
Use a scale of 1 cm to 5 km.

b Would you get a phone signal if you stood in the middle of the triangle?

8 Sketch each of these situations. Use angle facts to
answer the questions.

a A ship sails from a port on a bearing of 065° for 20 km.
On what bearing must it travel to return to the port?

b A plane flies from an airport on a bearing of 250° for 80 km.
On what bearing must it travel to return to the airport?

9 **Reasoning** Work out the length marked x on the diagram.

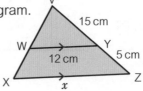

First show that the
two triangles VWY
and VXZ are similar.

10 **Reasoning** X is the centre of the regular pentagon ABCDE.
Explain why the five triangles are congruent.

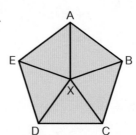

1 The scale on a diagram is 1 cm to 20 m.
   Calculate the real-life distance of these lengths on the diagram.

   a 5 cm ....

   b 10 cm ....

   c 0.5 cm ....

2 A map uses a scale of 1 cm to 50 m.
   What length on the map represents a real-life distance of

   a 100 m ....

   b 700 m ....

   c 1 km? ....

3 A ship sails 40 km from a port on a bearing of 070°.
   It then changes course and sails for 30 km on a bearing of 130°.

   a Use a scale of 1 cm to 10 km to draw an accurate scale drawing of the journey of the ship.

   b How far away is the ship from its
   starting point? ....

   c On what bearing should the ship sail to return to
   the port? ....

4 Triangles A, B and C are all congruent.

   a Work out the missing sides and angles.

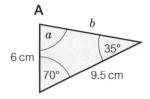
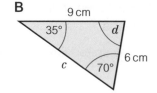
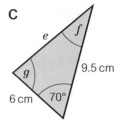

   b Explain why triangle D is not congruent to the others.

   D

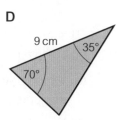

5 **a** Calculate the length BE.

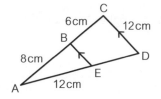

   b Calculate the length DE.

1 Work out the average speed for each journey.

a A train travels 240 miles in 3 hours.

b A cyclist travels 60 km in $2\frac{1}{2}$ hours.

c An athlete runs 1500 m in 240 seconds.

> When compound measures involve dividing by a unit of time, they are called **rates of change**. Speed is the rate of change of distance with time.

> Most objects do not travel at a constant speed. You usually calculate average speed over a whole journey: average speed = $\dfrac{\text{distance travelled}}{\text{time taken}}$

2 **Real** In 2009 Usain Bolt broke the 100 m world record.
He ran 100 m at an average speed of 10.48 m/s.
Find the time taken for him to run 100 m.
Round your answer to 2 decimal places.

> **Literacy hint**
>
> m/s means 'metres per second'.

Guided

3 Convert each speed into m/s.

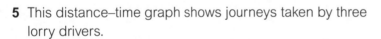

a 54 km/h

    54 × 1000 = 54 000

    54 km/h = 54 000 m/h

    54 000 ÷ 3600 = ...

    54 000 m/h = ... m/s

> Start by converting 54 km into m. You now have the speed in metres per hour.

> To convert between compound measures, convert each unit one at a time.

> There are 60 × 60 = 3600 seconds in 1 hour. Divide the speed in metres per hour by 3600 to find the speed in metres per second.

> **Worked example**
>
>

b 81 km/h   **c** 135 km/h

4 **Problem-solving / Reasoning** The speed limit on a motorway is 70 mph.
A cheetah can run 200 m in 7 seconds.

Can a cheetah exceed the motorway speed limit? Show working to explain your answer.

5 This distance–time graph shows journeys taken by three lorry drivers.

a Which driver travelled at the fastest speed at any time?

b Which driver had the highest average speed for the entire journey?

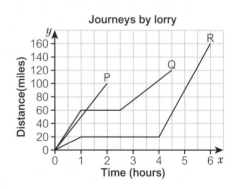

Journeys by lorry

A fourth driver completes the same trip as driver R in a total time of 5 hours. She travels at a constant speed for the whole journey.

c Calculate her constant speed.

Check Tick each box as your **confidence** in this topic improves.   **Need extra help?** Go to page 87 and tick the boxes next to Q1–3. Then try them once you've finished 9.1–9.3.

84

1 STEM / Real As part of a science experiment, Luis measures the mass and volume of samples of four different metals. He records his results in this table.

Metal	Volume (cm³)	Mass (g)
iron	142	1118
copper	18	160
gold	0.25	4.8

Calculate the density of each metal, giving your answers in g/cm³ correct to 1 decimal place.

> **Density** is a compound measure. Density measures the mass per unit of volume. Density is often measured in grams per cubic centimetre (g/cm³) and kilograms per cubic metre (kg/m³). The Greek letter ρ (rho) is used to represent density.
>
> density $(\rho) = \dfrac{\text{mass}}{\text{volume}}$

Worked example

 2 STEM The table shows the densities of three types of wood. Calculate

a the volume of 200 kg of balsa

$$\text{volume} = \frac{\text{mass}}{\text{density}}$$
$$= \frac{200}{160}$$
$$= \ldots\ldots\ldots \text{ m}^3$$

> Rearrange the formula density $= \dfrac{\text{mass}}{\text{volume}}$ to make volume the subject.

> The unit of density is kg/m³ and the unit of mass is kg, so the unit of volume is m³.

b the mass of 2.5 m³ of ebony   **c** the mass of 36 cm³ of oak.

Wood	Density, ρ (kg/m³)
balsa	160
ebony	1200
oak	740

> The density is given in kg/m³ so you need to convert cm³ to m³.

 3 A force of 55 N is applied to an area of 15 cm². Calculate the pressure. Give your answer to 1 decimal place.

 4 Real At a depth of 300 m, the water pressure is 294 N/cm². Calculate the force applied to the hull of a submarine with a surface area of 1600 m².

> **Strategy hint**
> Make sure all the area measures are in the same units.

> **Pressure** is a compound measure. Pressure is the force applied over a given area. The most common units of pressure are newtons per square centimetre (N/cm²) and newtons per square metre (N/m²).
>
> pressure $= \dfrac{\text{force}}{\text{area}}$ or $P = \dfrac{F}{A}$

 5 STEM / Problem-solving Objects that are less dense than their surroundings float.
The density of water at 4°C is 1 g/cm³.

a Will this cuboid, which has a mass of 18.8 g, float in a bowl of water with a temperature of 4°C?

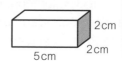
5 cm, 2 cm, 2 cm

b The density of petrol at 60°F is 0.737 g/cm³. Will the cuboid in part **a** float in petrol at 60°F?

Check Tick each box as your **confidence** in this topic improves.

Need extra help? Go to page 87 and tick the boxes next to Q4 and 5. Then try them once you've finished 9.1–9.3.

85

Guided

1 Write down the upper and lower bounds for each measurement.

> When a measurement is rounded, the actual value could be bigger or smaller than the rounded value. The biggest possible actual value is called the **upper bound**. The smallest possible actual value is called the **lower bound**.

a The page of a book is 18 cm wide, to the nearest cm.

Upper bound = 18.5 cm — Any number less than 18.5 is rounded to 18.

Lower bound = 17.5 cm — Any number greater than or equal to 17.5 is rounded to 18.

b The Kara Crater in Russia is 65 km wide, to the nearest km.

c The mass of a book is 290.4 g, to 1 decimal place.

> The upper bound is half a measure greater than the rounded value. The lower bound is half a measure less than the rounded value.

2 There were 83 000 people at a football match, rounded to the nearest thousand. Write down the upper and lower bounds for the number of people at the match.

> The number of people is a discrete measurement. This means it must be a whole number. Work out the largest possible whole number that rounds to 83 000, to the nearest thousand.

 3 **Problem-solving** A bag contains 100 g of sweets, correct to the nearest 10 g. The bag costs £1.20. Calculate (in pence)

a the greatest possible cost per g

b the least possible cost per g.

Guided

4 **Real** The world record for the 400 metres was broken in 1999 with a time of 43.18 seconds to 2 decimal places. Complete this inequality to show the upper and lower bounds of the time.

> You can use inequalities to show upper and lower bounds for continuous measurements like time, length or mass.

.... $\leq t <$ .... — What is half a measure?

5 **Problem-solving** A recipe makes 600 ml of lemonade, correct to the nearest 10 ml. The lemonade is divided equally between 3 glasses. Calculate the maximum absolute error for the amount of lemonade in each glass.

> The **absolute error** is the maximum difference between the measured value and the actual value. The symbol ± means 'plus or minus'. You can use it to show the absolute error in a measurement.

6 **Real** A section of wooden flooring is 190 mm wide, to the nearest 10 mm. 12 sections of flooring are joined together side by side.

a Write down the upper and lower bounds for the width of one section of flooring.

b Work out the upper and lower bounds for the total width of the flooring.

c Work out the absolute error for the total width of the flooring

---

Check Tick each box as your **confidence** in this topic improves.

Need extra help? Go to page 88 and tick the boxes next to Q6–9. Then try them once you've finished 9.1–9.3.

Rates of change

1 Find the average speed for each journey. Give units with your answers.

    a A cyclist completes a 35-mile race in 2 hours.

    b A coach travels 300 miles in 6 hours.

You can use the formula triangle for speed.
The position of the variables tells you whether to multiply or divide.

$d = s \times t$

$s = \dfrac{d}{t}$ $t = \dfrac{d}{s}$

2 An athlete completes a 5000 m race at an average speed of 5 m/s. Calculate the time taken in minutes and seconds.

3 The distance–time graph shows three stages of a journey of a car.

    a Which stage of the car journey shows the highest average speed?

    b What is the speed for this part of the journey in km/h?

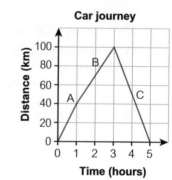

Density and pressure

4 Calculate the density of each material. Give units with your answers.

    a A bronze statue with a mass of 1.4 kg and a volume of 0.175 m³.

    b A gold ring with a mass of 14.49 g and a volume 0.75 cm³.

You can use the formula triangle for density.

mass = density × volume

density = $\dfrac{\text{mass}}{\text{volume}}$

volume = $\dfrac{\text{mass}}{\text{density}}$

5 A force of 1080 N is applied to an area of 450 cm². Calculate the pressure in N/cm².

This is the formula triangle for pressure.

Upper and lower bounds

6 Write the upper and lower bounds for each measurement.

a The Shard in London is 308 m high, correct to the nearest m.

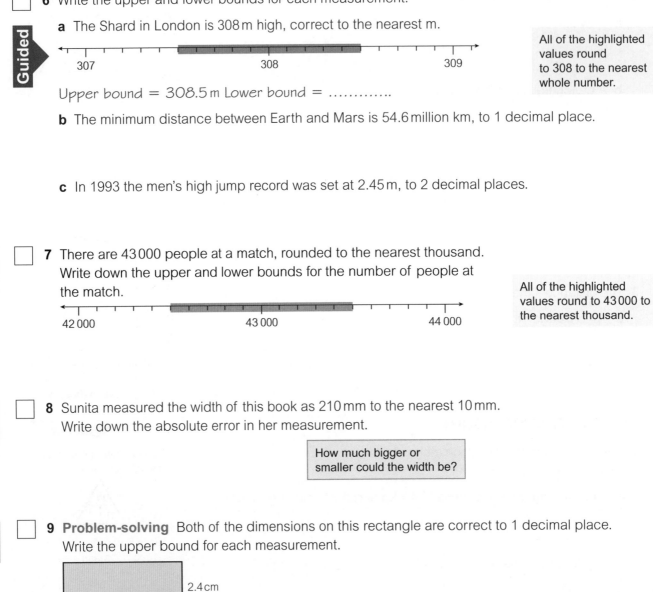

All of the highlighted values round to 308 to the nearest whole number.

Upper bound = 308.5 m   Lower bound = ...

b The minimum distance between Earth and Mars is 54.6 million km, to 1 decimal place.

c In 1993 the men's high jump record was set at 2.45 m, to 2 decimal places.

7 There are 43 000 people at a match, rounded to the nearest thousand. Write down the upper and lower bounds for the number of people at the match.

All of the highlighted values round to 43 000 to the nearest thousand.

8 Sunita measured the width of this book as 210 mm to the nearest 10 mm. Write down the absolute error in her measurement.

How much bigger or smaller could the width be?

9 **Problem-solving** Both of the dimensions on this rectangle are correct to 1 decimal place. Write the upper bound for each measurement.

2.4 cm

3.9 cm

1 A circle has a radius of 150 mm, correct to the nearest 5 mm.
Write down the upper and lower bounds for the radius of the circle.

2 The upper and lower bounds for the weight, x kg, of a whale are given as $3950 \leqslant x < 4050$.
Work out the degree of accuracy that the whale was weighed to.

3 **Problem-solving** A platinum nugget (lump) has a mass of 1.3 kg. The density of platinum is 21.5 g/cm³.
What is the volume of the platinum nugget?
Give your answer correct to 3 significant figures.

4 **Modelling / Problem-solving** This paddling pool is filled from a hosepipe connected to a tap with a flow rate of 20 litres per minute. Model the paddling pool as a cylinder and estimate the length of time it will take to fill three-quarters of the paddling pool.

1 litre = ☐ cm³

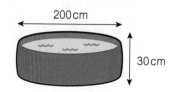

5 **Problem-solving / STEM** This solid brass block has a density of 8.6 g/cm³.

a Calculate the mass of the block in kilograms.

b Calculate the weight of the block in newtons.

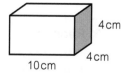

| **Literacy hint** |
| The weight of an object is the force due to gravity. On Earth, weight = mass × 9.8. |

c The block is positioned as shown.
Calculate the pressure exerted by the block on the ground.

The block is rotated so that one of its square faces rests on the ground.

d Calculate the pressure exerted by the block on the ground in this position.

6 A bag of rice has a mass of 1 kg, to the nearest 10 g.

    a Write the absolute error for the mass of the bag in the form 1000 g ± ☐

    b Calculate the absolute error for the mass of 12 bags of rice.

    One bag of rice is divided equally into 8 individual portions.

    c Calculate the absolute error for the mass of rice in each portion.

7 Reasoning A car travels at an average speed of 70 km/h for 3 hours.
It then travels at an average speed of 85 km/h for 2 hours.
Work out the average speed of the car over the entire journey.

8 Reasoning A four-legged table has a mass of 20 kg.
A box of mass 40 kg is placed on the table.
The pressure acting on the base of each of the legs is 14 700 N/m².
What is the area of the bottom of each leg of the table?

> Use weight = mg
> where g = 9.8 m/s².

1 The mass of an egg is 62 g to the nearest gram. Write down

   a the upper bound for the mass of the egg ....

   b the lower bound for the mass of the egg. ....

2 The capacity, C, of a bottle is 500 ml, to the nearest 10 ml.
   Complete the inequality .... ml ⩽ .... < .... ml

3 A train travels 150 miles in 1 hour and 40 minutes.
   Calculate the average speed of the train in miles per hour.

4 Convert 15 m/s into km/h.

5 This triangular prism has a mass of 7.4 kg.
   Calculate the density of the material used to make the
   triangular prism.
   Give your answer in g/cm³ correct to 1 decimal place.

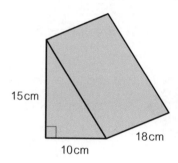

15 cm
10 cm
18 cm

6 Calculate the pressure that the triangular prism in Q5 exerts on a
   surface when it is positioned as shown.
   Give your answer correct to 3 significant figures.

   Take the acceleration due
   to gravity to be 9.8 m/s².

7 A fence is made by joining together 5 identical panels.
   Each panel has a length of 240 cm, correct to the nearest 10 cm.
   Calculate the lower bound for the length of the fence.

Guided

1 Draw these graphs from their equations.

a $y = 2x + 1$

b $y = x - 3$

c $y = -x - 1$

d $y = -3x - 3$

e $y = \frac{1}{2}x - 4$

f $y = -\frac{1}{2}x - 2$

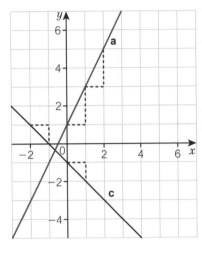

Plot the y-intercept. Decide if the gradient is positive or negative. Draw a line with this gradient, starting from the y-intercept. Extend your line right across the grid. Label the line.

What do you know about the gradients of parallel lines?

2 Without drawing the graphs, sort these equations into pairs of parallel lines.

A $y = 3x + 3$ B $y = \frac{1}{4}x + 1$ C $y = 2x$

D $y = 0.25x - 3$ E $y = 3x - 1.5$ F $y = 2x - 8$

Guided

3 Plot and label the graph of $3x + 2y = 9$.

When $x = 0$

$3 \times 0 + 2y = 9$

$2y = 9$

$y = \ldots\ldots$

To find the y-intercept, substitute $x = 0$ into the equation. Solve to find the value of y.

When $y = 0$

$3x + 2 \times 0 = 9$

$3x = 9$

$x = \ldots\ldots$

To find the x-intercept, substitute $y = 0$ into the equation. Solve to find the value of x.

x	0	
y		0

Draw a table of values with $x = 0$ and $y = 0$.

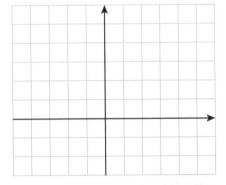

Worked example

4 On the grid in Q3, plot and label the graph of $2x - y = -5$.

5 Which is the steepest line?

A $y = 3x - 2$ B $8x + 4y = 6$ C $5x - y = 12$

To compare the gradients of two straight lines, their equations need to be in the form $y = mx + c$. Make y the subject. Write the x-term first on the right-hand side.

6 Which of these lines pass through $(0, -4)$? Show how you worked it out.

A $y = -4x + 2$ B $y = 2x - 4$ C $5x + 2y = -8$ D $3x + y = 4$

Check   Tick each box as your **confidence** in this topic improves.

☹ 😐 ☺

Need extra help? Go to page 100 and tick the box next to Q12. Then try it once you've finished 10.1–10.6.

Graphs of quadratic functions

1 Reasoning

Guided

a Complete the table of values for $y = x^2$.

x	−3	−2	−1	0	1	2	3
y	9	4					

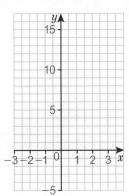

A **quadratic function** contains a term in x^2 but no higher power of x. $y = x^2$, $y = 5x^2$, $y = x^2 + 5$ and $y = x^2 + 3x + 2$ are all quadratic. The graph of a quadratic function is called a **parabola**.

b Plot the coordinates from your table of values for $y = x^2$.
Join the points to make a smooth curve.
Label your graph $y = x^2$.

c Complete the table of values for the quadratic function $y = x^2 + 5$.

x	−3	−2	−1	0	1	2	3
y							

d Plot the graph of $y = x^2 + 5$ on the same axes. Label your graph with its equation.

e What is the same about the two graphs? ....

f What is different about the two graphs? ....

g Predict what the graph of $y = x^2 − 5$ looks like.
Plot the graph on the same axes to test your prediction.

2 Reasoning

a Complete this table of values for the quadratic function $y = 3x^2$.

x	−4	−3	−2	−1	0	1	2	3	4
y									

b Plot and label the graphs of these quadratic functions on the axes.
i $y = x^2$ **ii** $y = 3x^2$ **iii** $y = \frac{1}{3}x^2$

c What is the same about the three graphs?

d What is different about the three graphs?

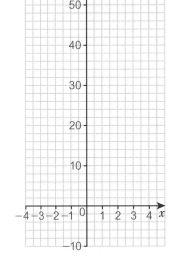

3 a Match each graph to its function.

i $y = x^2$ ....
ii $y = 3x^2$ ....
iii $y = −3x^2 + 5$ ....
iv $y = −3x^2$ ....
v $y = −x^2$ ....
vi $y = −x^2 + 5$ ....

A **turning point** of a graph is where its direction changes. A turning point can be a maximum or minimum point. A **maximum** is the point on the graph with the greatest y-coordinate. A **minimum** is the point on the graph with the lowest y-coordinate.

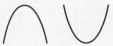

maximum   minimum

b Under each graph, write the coordinates of its turning point and whether it is a maximum or a minimum.

Check   Tick each box as your **confidence** in this topic improves.

Need extra help? Go to pages 98 and 99 and tick the boxes next to Q1–4. Then try them once you've finished 10.1–10.6.

Guided

1 Solve these pairs of simultaneous equations.

a $4x + y = 33$ and $y = 2x$

$4x + y = 33$ (1) — Write one equation above the other with the equals signs lined up. Number them (1) and (2).

$y = 2x$ (2)

$4x + 2x = 33$ — Substitute $y = 2x$ into equation (1).

$6x = 33$ — Simplify and solve.

$x = 5.5$

$y = 2 \times 5.5$ — Substitute the value of x into one equation.

$y = \ldots\ldots\ldots$

Check: $4x + y = 33$ (1)

$4 \times 5.5 + \ldots\ldots = \ldots\ldots$ — Check the values in the other equation.

Literacy hint

Solve means work out the values for x and y.

You can solve two **simultaneous equations** to find the values of two variables.

b $5x + y = 72$ and $y = 4x$ **c** $6x + y = 26$ and $y = 2x$ **d** $2x + y = 28$ and $y = 3x$

Guided

2 Solve these pairs of simultaneous equations.

a $4x + y = 23$ and $x - y = 2$

$4x + y = 23$ (1) — Write one equation above the other with the equals signs lined up. Number them.

$+ \; x - y = 2$ (2)

$5x + 0 = 25$ (1) + (2) — Add equations (1) and (2) together to cancel y. Solve for x.

$x = 5$

$5 - y = 2$ — Substitute $x = 5$ into one equation to work out y.

$y = \ldots\ldots\ldots$

Check: $4x + y = 23$ (1)

$4 \times 5 + \ldots\ldots = \ldots\ldots$ — Substitute both values into the other equation to check.

b $5x + y = 39$ and $3x - y = 17$

3 Solve these pairs of simultaneous equations.

a $3x + 2y = 16$ and $5x + 2y = 24$

Strategy hint

Subtract one equation from the other to eliminate one of the variables.

b $5x + 2y = 39$ and $3x + 2y = 25$

Check   Tick each box as your **confidence** in this topic improves.

Need extra help? Go to page 99 and tick the boxes next to Q5–7. Then try them once you've finished 10.1–10.6.

1 a Draw the graph of $6x + 2y = 18$.

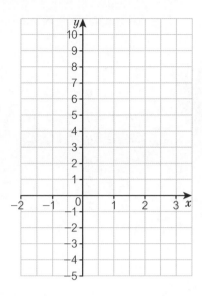

b Use your graph to write down the gradient and y-intercept.

c Write the equation of the line as $y = mx + c$.

d Rearrange $6x + 2y = 18$ to make y the subject.
What do you notice?

2 a Write each equation in the form $y = mx + c$.

i $y - 5x = 2$ **ii** $4y - 3x = 7$ **iii** $\frac{1}{2}y + 3x = 4$

b Which line has the steepest gradient? ....

3 Decide whether each pair of lines have the same y-intercept.

To compare two lines, write their equations in the form $y = mx + c$.

a $y - 5 = 3x$ and $y + 2x = 5$ **b** $x + y = -6$ and $5x + 2y = -12$

4 Find the equation of the line that passes through each pair of points.

Guided

a A(2, 2) and B(5, 14)

$y = mx + c$

At A, $x = 2$ and $y = 2$

Points A and B lie on the line, so their coordinates satisfy the equation of the line. Substitute the x- and y-values from point A into $y = mx + c$ and write an equation for the line.

$2 = m \times 2 + c$

$2 = 2m + c$

At B, $x = 5$ and $y = 14$

Substitute the x- and y-values from point B into $y = mx + c$.

$14 = m \times 5 + c$

$14 = 5m + c$

$14 = 5m + c$ (1)

$-2 = 2m + c$ (2)

Solve the simultaneous equations to find m and c. To eliminate c, subtract equation (1) from equation (2).

$12 = 3m$ (2) − (1)

$m = ...$

Substitute $m = \square$ into equation (1).

$2 = 2 \times .... + c$

$c = ...$

Substitute the values of m and c into $y = mx + c$.

Equation of line is $y = ...$

b P(9, 8) and Q(2, −6)

More simultaneous equations

Guided

1 Solve these pairs of simultaneous equations.

a $3x + y = 30$
   $x + 2y = 25$

   $3x + y = 30$ (1)
   $x + 2y = 25$ (2)
   $6x + 2y = 60$ (3)
   $-x + 2y = 25$
   $5x + 0 = 35$ (3) − (2)
   $x = 7$
   $3 \times \text{.......} + y = 30$
   $y = \text{.................}$
   Check: $7 + 2 \times \text{......} = \text{......}$
   Solution is $x = \text{.......}$ and $y = \text{.......}$

> First write the equations one under the other and label them (1) and (2). Adding or subtracting will not eliminate either x or y.

> Multiply equation (1) by 2 so that it has the same y-coefficient as equation (2).

> Subtract one equation from the other.

> Substitute your value for x into equation (1).

> Check that your values for x and y work in equation (2).

b $2x + y = 18$
   $x + 3y = 29$

c $5x - y = 13$
   $x + 3y = 25$

d $x - 3y = 5$
   $7x + y = 79$

e $8x + y = 34$
   $x + 5y = 53$

Worked example

2 Solve these pairs of simultaneous equations.

a $3x + y = 41$
   $4x + 3y = 63$

b $4x - y = 24$
   $5x + 2y = 43$

c $5x + 2y = 52$
   $9x - 4y = 10$

> Multiply one of the equations. Do you need to add or subtract?

Check   Tick each box as your **confidence** in this topic improves.

☹ 😐 ☺

Need extra help? Go to page 99 and tick the boxes next to Q8 and 9. Then try them once you've finished 10.1–10.6.

96

Graphs and simultaneous equations

1 Draw graphs to solve this pair of simultaneous equations.

$$2x - y = 5$$
$$x + y = 4$$

> The point where two (or more) lines cross is called the **point of intersection**.

$$2x - y = 5$$

> Rearrange the equations in the form $y = mx + c$ and then draw and label the graphs.

$$y = 2x - 5$$

$$x + y = 4$$

> You can find the solution to a pair of simultaneous equations by
> • drawing the lines on a coordinate grid
> • finding the point of intersection.

$$y = \ldots\ldots\ldots\ldots$$

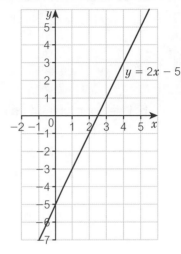

The lines intersect

at (......., ...)

Solution is $x = $ .... and $y = $ ....

2 **Real / Modelling** Two families visit a zoo.

The entrance costs are:
Smith family: 3 adults and 2 children cost £78.
Jones family: 2 adults and 5 children cost £96.

a Write down two equations to model these situations.

b Draw graphs to model the simultaneous equations in part **a**.

c Write down the cost of an adult ticket and the cost of a child ticket.

3 Here is a graph of two equations.
Write down the solutions to the simultaneous equations.

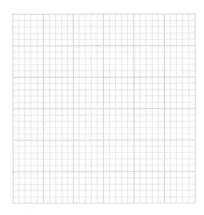

4 **Reasoning / Problem-solving** The quadratic graph in Q3 is the graph of $y = -x^2 + 3$.

a Write down the equation of a line that will never intersect $y = -x^2 + 3$.

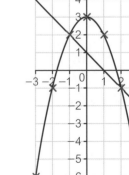

b Show algebraically that the two graphs will not cross.

Check Tick each box as your **confidence** in this topic improves. ☹ 😐 ☺ ☐ ☐ ☐

Need extra help? Go to page 100 and tick the box next to Q12. Then try it once you've finished 10.1–10.6.

Quadratic graphs

Guided

1 a Complete this table of values for the function $y = 2x^2$.

x	−3	−2	−1	0	1	2	3
x^2	9						
$y = 2x^2$	18						

x	−3
x^2	−3 × −3 = 9
$y = 2x^2$	2 × 9 = 18

b Use your table of values to write down each pair of coordinates.
(−3, 18), ...

c Plot and label the graph of the function $y = 2x^2$ on these axes.

d What are the coordinates of the turning point of the graph? ....

e Is the turning point a minimum or maximum point? ....

The turning point of the graph is the lowest point.

(☐ , ☐)

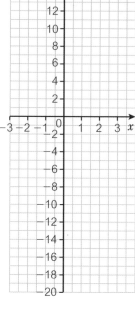

2 a Use your table in Q1 to complete this table of values for the function $y = -2x^2$.

x	−3	−2	−1	0	1	2	3
$2x^2$	18						
$y = -2x^2$	−18						

Draw each graph using a different colour.

b Plot and label the graph of $y = -2x^2$ on the same axes as in Q1.

c What are the coordinates of the turning point of the graph? ....

d What transformation maps the graph of $y = 2x^2$ to the graph of $y = -2x^2$?

Could you
- reflect it
- rotate it about a point
- translate it?

3 Reasoning

a Complete this table of values for the function $y = x^2 + 8$.

x	−3	−2	−1	0	1	2	3
x^2							
$y = x^2 + 8$							

b Plot the points and join them with a smooth curve. Label your graph $y = x^2 + 8$.

c i What are the coordinates of the minimum point? ....

ii How can you tell the coordinates of the minimum point by looking at the function $y = x^2 + 8$?

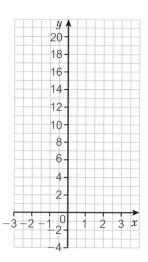

d What are the coordinates of the minimum point of each of these?

i $y = x^2 + 3$ ....

ii $y = x^2 + 10$ ....

4 Match each function to its graph.

   i $y = x^2 + 3$ ....   **ii** $y = 2x^2 + 7$ ....

   iii $y = x^2$ ....   **iv** $y = -2x^2$ ....

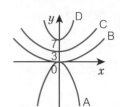

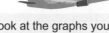

Look at the graphs you have already drawn.

Simultaneous equations

5 Find the values of x and y that satisfy these pairs of equations.

Guided

  a $6x + y = 11$

      $y = 5x$

      $6x + y = 11$

      $6x + 5x = 11$

        $11x = 11$

          $x = $ ....

   $y = 5 \times$ .... = ...

   Check: ....

> $y = 5x$, so substitute y with $5x$.

> Substitute your value for x into one of the equations.

  b $2x + y = 20$

      $y = \frac{1}{2}x$

  c $5x + y = 16$

      $y = 3x$

6 $5x + y = 41$ and $3x - y = 15$ are a pair of simultaneous equations.

  a Add the two equations together.

  b What happens to the y terms? Explain.

  c Solve your equation to work out x.

  d Using the value of x, find the value of y.

$$5x + y = 41$$
$$+ \; 3x - y = 15$$

7 $5x + y = 67$ and $3x + y = 43$ are a pair of simultaneous equations.

  a Subtract one equation from the other.

  b What happens to the y terms? Explain.

  c Solve your equation to work out x.

  d Using the value of x, find the value of y.

$$5x + y = 67$$
$$- \; 3x + y = 43$$

Worked example

8 $6x + y = 18$ and $x + 3y = 20$ are a pair of simultaneous equations.

  a Multiply all the terms in the first equation by 3. Then subtract one equation from the other and solve.

  b Solve the pair of simultaneous equations again. This time multiply all the terms in the second equation by 6. Then subtract one equation from the other and solve.

9 **Real / Problem-solving** 5 gold bars and 4 silver bars weigh 66 kg.
1 gold bar and 10 silver bars weigh 22.4 kg.
What is the weight of 1 gold bar and the weight of 1 silver bar?

First construct a pair of simultaneous equations.

Straight-line graphs

☐ **10 a** Write each equation in the form $y = mx + c$.

  i $y - 7x = 2$ **ii** $3y - 9x = 6$ **iii** $2y - 8x = 10$

> Rearrange the equation to make y the subject. In the form $y = mx + c$, m is the gradient and c is the y-intercept.

  b Write down the gradient and the y-intercept for each equation.

☐ **11 a** Complete the table.

Guided

  b Write down the equations of the lines that are parallel.

  c Write down the equations of the lines that have the same y-intercept.

$y = mx + c$	Gradient m	y-intercept $(0, c)$
$y = 2x + 6$	2	$(0, 6)$
$y = -4x + 1$		
$y = 2x + 1$		
$y = \frac{1}{4}x - 7$		

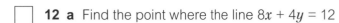

> Parallel lines have the same ....
> Positive gradients slope uphill left to right. ╱
> Negative gradients slope downhill left to right. ╲

☐ **12 a** Find the point where the line $8x + 4y = 12$

  i crosses the y-axis   **ii** crosses the x-axis.

> The line crosses the y-axis at $(0, \square)$.
> For each point, substitute the value you know into the equation.

  b Plot the points you found in part **a**, and join them with a straight line.

  c Plot the graph of $6x - 2y = 4$.

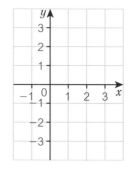

  d Write down the point of intersection of these simultaneous equations. ....

☐ **13** Tariq finds the equation of the line between points $(3, 7)$ and $(5, 11)$.

Guided

  a Complete his working.

  At $(3, 7)$, $x = $ .... and $y = $ ....

  Substitute into $y = mx + c$

  .... $= $ .... $m + c$ (1)

  b Write another equation using the point $(5, 11)$.
     Label the equation (2).

  c Solve the simultaneous equations to work out m and c.

  d Write the equation of the line.

1 The total surface area, A, of a hemisphere of radius r cm is given by $A = 3\pi r^2$.

a Use the grid to plot the graph of A for $r = 0$ to 3.

> Make a table using at least 4 values of r between 0 and 3.

b Use your graph to estimate

   i the total surface area of a hemisphere with radius 1.5 cm.

   ii the radius of a hemisphere with total surface area 50 cm².

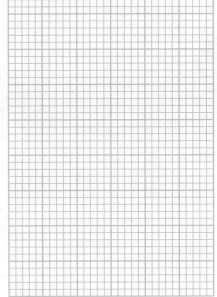

2 Find the values of x and y that satisfy these pairs of equations.

   a $7x + y = 8$

   $\quad y = -3x$

   b $5x - y = -27$

   $\quad y = -4x$

> Take care when multiplying and dividing with positives and negatives.

3 Work out the equation of the line between the points $(-9, -8)$ and $(-7, -15)$.

4 Problem-solving The perimeter of this rectangle is 30 cm.

   a Find a formula for the area A of the rectangle in terms of w.

w	Perimeter = 30 cm

   b Plot the graph of A for $w = 0$ to 15.

   c Use your graph to estimate

      i the maximum possible area of the rectangle

      ii the dimensions of the rectangle when the area is 40 cm².

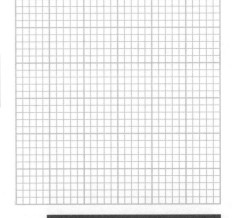

> **Strategy hint**
>
> Write an expression for the length, l, of the rectangle using the formula for the perimeter.

5 a Factorise the expression $x^2 - 4$ using the difference of two squares.

   b Use your factorisation to sketch the graph of $y = x^2 - 4$. On your sketch, mark

      i the point where the graph crosses the y-axis

      ii the coordinates of the turning point.

   c Sketch the graph of $y = x^2 - 9$.

6 Solve this pair of simultaneous equations.

$2x + 5y = 37$ (1)

$5x + 7y = 65$ (2)

$10x + 25y = 185$ (3) — Multiply equation (1) by 5. Label it (3).

$10x + 14y = 130$ (4) — Multiply equation (2) by 2. Label it (4).

$11y = $ .... — Work out equation (3) − equation (4).

$y = $ .... — Work out the values of x and y.

Worked example

Simultaneous equations can have no solutions, one solution or infinitely many solutions.

No solution   One solution   Infinitely many solutions

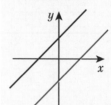 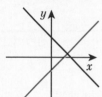 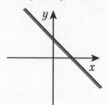

7 Reasoning Use algebra to decide whether each pair of equations has no solution, one solution or infinitely many solutions. If possible, find the values of x and y that satisfy each pair of equations.

a $x - y = 2$
$4x - y = -7$

b $3x + 5y = 7$
$6x + 10y = 14$

c $4x - 3y = 15$
$7x - 5y = 25$

8 Real / Modelling At a fund-raising event, students sell cakes and biscuits.
In the first hour, they sell 80 cakes and 50 biscuits for £75.
In the second hour, they sell 56 cakes and 120 biscuits for £78.
Work out the cost of 1 cake and the cost of 1 biscuit.

9 Problem-solving Use simultaneous equations to work out the values of a and b.

a
15 cm

Area = 99 cm²
b | Perimeter = 46 cm | a

3 cm ↕ 7 cm
8 cm

b

$3a + 2b$
125°
131°
$2a + 3b$

Use the information to form a pair of simultaneous equations. Then solve the equations to find a and b.

1 **a** Complete this table of values for the function $y = 2x^2 - 3$.

x	-3	-2	-1	0	1	2	3
y							

b Plot the graph of $y = 2x^2 - 3$ on the grid.

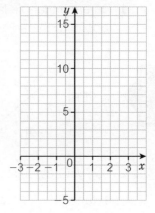

2 For each equation write down **i** the gradient **ii** the y-intercept.

a $y = 2x + 9$ **b** $y = \frac{1}{2}x - 5$

3 Work out the equation of the line between points (6, 8) and (9, 20).

4 Find the values of x and y that satisfy these pairs of equations.

a $3x + y = 33$ **b** $5x + 3y = 41$ **c** $7x + 4y = 50$
 $x - y = 7$ $8x - 3y = 11$ $7x + 6y = 68$

5 **a** Draw the graph of $2x - y = 1$.

b Use your graph to solve the simultaneous equations $2x - y = 1$ and $y = 4$.

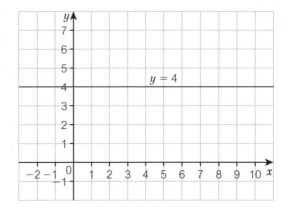

6 A hire company charges per day with a fixed deposit.
When Lali hires a carpet cleaner for 3 days, her bill is $79.
When Sayyid hires a carpet cleaner for 7 days, his bill is $151.
Let x represent the cost per day and y represent the deposit.

a Write an equation for Lali. ....

b Write an equation for Sayyid. ....

c Find the values of x and y that satisfy this pair of equations.

1 On each triangle label the hypotenuse 'hyp', the opposite side to angle θ 'opp' and the adjacent side to angle θ 'adj'.

a

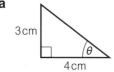

b

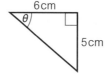

c

> The side opposite the chosen angle (angle θ in this diagram) is called the **opposite** side. The side next to θ is called the **adjacent** side.
>
>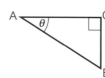

2 Use your calculator to find, correct to 1 d.p.

a $\tan 65°$.................

b $\tan 38°$.................

3 Write $\tan \theta$ as a fraction for each triangle.

a

3 cm
4 cm

b

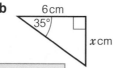

6 cm
5 cm

c

5 cm
7 cm

> The ratio of the opposite side to the adjacent side is called the **tangent** of the angle.
> The tangent of angle θ is written as **tan θ**.
> $\tan \theta = \dfrac{\text{opposite}}{\text{adjacent}}$

4 Use the tangent ratio to work out the value of x, correct to 1 d.p.

a

x cm
50°
4 cm

b

6 cm
35°
x cm

> Write the tangent ratio.

$\tan \theta = \dfrac{\text{opposite}}{\text{adjacent}}$

> Identify the opposite and adjacent sides.

opposite = x, adjacent = 4, $\theta = 50°$

$\tan 50° = \dfrac{x}{4}$

> Substitute the sides and angle into the equation.

.... $\times \tan 50° = x$

> Rearrange to make x the subject.
> Use your calculator to work out ☐ $\times \tan 50°$.

x = ... cm (to 1 d.p.)

c

5 cm
58°
x cm

d

7 cm
62°
x cm

e

x cm
53°
12 cm

> **Worked example**
>
>

opp = 7, adj = x, $\theta = 62°$

$\tan 62° = \dfrac{7}{x}$

$x = \dfrac{..........}{........}$

> Rearrange the formula to make x the subject.

x = ...

Check Tick each box as your **confidence** in this topic improves.

😟 😐 😊

☐ ☐ ☐

Need extra help? Go to pages 109 and 110 and tick the boxes next to Q1–3 and 5. Then try them once you've finished 11.1–11.5.

1 Use your calculator to find, correct to 1 d.p.

a sin 56° .... **b** sin 21° .... **c** sin 85° ....

On your calculator, enter

2 Write sin θ as a fraction for each triangle.

a 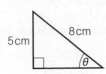 **b**   **c**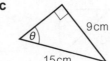

The ratio of the opposite side to the hypotenuse is called the **sine** of the angle. The sine of angle θ is written as **sin** θ.

$$\sin \theta = \frac{\text{opposite}}{\text{hypotenuse}}$$

3 Use the sine ratio to work out the value of x, correct to 1 d.p.

a

b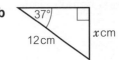

Guided

$\sin \theta = \dfrac{opposite}{hypotenuse}$ — Write the sine ratio.

opposite = x, hypotenuse = 6, $\theta = 48°$ — Identify the opposite side and hypotenuse.

$\sin 48° = \dfrac{x}{6}$ — Substitute the sides and angle into the equation.

.... $\times \sin 48° = x$ — Rearrange to make x the subject. Use your calculator to work out ☐ × sin 48°.

$x = ...$ cm (to 1 d.p.)

c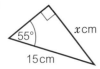

d

opp = 5, hyp = x, $\theta = 58°$

$\sin 58° = \dfrac{5}{x}$ — Rearrange the formula to make x the subject.

$x = \dfrac{.........}{........}$

$x = ...$

e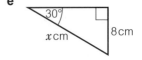

4 Problem-solving / Reasoning For each triangle

  i decide whether you need to use the tangent or the sine ratio   **ii** work out the value of p.

a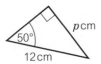

b

Check Tick each box as your **confidence** in this topic improves. ☹ 😐 ☺

Need extra help? Go to pages 109 and 110 and tick the boxes next to Q2–5. Then try them once you've finished 11.1–11.5.

105

1 Use your calculator to find, correct to 1 d.p.

   a $\cos 24°$................. **b** $\cos 85°$.................   **c** $\cos 48°$.................   **d** $\cos 15°$.................

2 Write $\cos \theta$ as a fraction for each triangle.

> The ratio of the adjacent side to the hypotenuse is called the **cosine** of the angle.
> The cosine of angle θ is written as $\cos \theta$.
>
> $\cos \theta = \dfrac{\text{adjacent}}{\text{hypotenuse}}$

  a   **b**   **c**

3 Use the cosine ratio to work out the value of x, correct to 1 d.p.

  a   **b**

Guided

$\cos \theta = \dfrac{\text{adjacent}}{\text{hypotenuse}}$ ——[Write the cosine ratio.]

adjacent $= x$, hypotenuse $= 8$, $\theta = 53°$ —[Identify the adjacent side and hypotenuse.]

$\cos 53° = \dfrac{x}{8}$ —[Substitute the sides and angle into the equation.]

.... $\times \cos 53° = x$ —[Rearrange to make x the subject. Use your calculator to work out $\square \times \cos 53°$.]

$x = $ .... cm (to 1 d.p.)

  c   **d**   **e**   **f**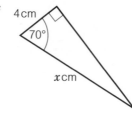

adj $= 9$, hyp $= x$, $\theta = 65°$

$\cos 65° = \dfrac{9}{x}$

[Rearrange the formula to make x the subject.] — $x = \dfrac{..........}{........}$

$x = $ ....

4 **Problem-solving / Reasoning** For each triangle

  i decide whether you need to use the tangent, sine or cosine ratio   **ii** work out the value of p.

  a    **b**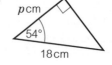

Check   Tick each box as your **confidence** in this topic improves.

Need extra help? Go to page 110 and tick the boxes next to Q2, 3 and 5. Then try them once you've finished 11.1–11.5.

106

Guided

1 a Use the sine ratio to work out the missing angles.

i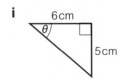

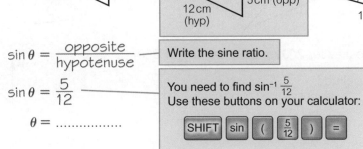

Label the sides.

Write the sine ratio.

$$\sin\theta = \frac{\text{opposite}}{\text{hypotenuse}}$$

$$\sin\theta = \frac{5}{12}$$

$$\theta = \text{................}$$

You need to find $\sin^{-1}\frac{5}{12}$
Use these buttons on your calculator:

SHIFT | sin | (| $\frac{5}{12}$ |) | =

ii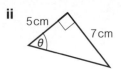

> You can use **inverse** trigonometric functions to work out unknown angles.
> $\cos\theta = x$, so $\theta = \cos^{-1}x$
> $\sin\theta = x$, so $\theta = \sin^{-1}x$
> $\tan\theta = x$, so $\theta = \tan^{-1}x$

Follow the same method as in part **a** but use the tangent ratio.

b Use the tangent ratio to work out the missing angles.

i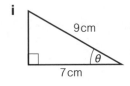

ii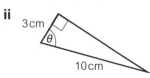

c Use the cosine ratio to work out the missing angles.

i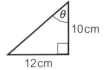

ii

Worked example

2 Work out the missing angle in each right-angled triangle

a

b

c

d

3 Real / Problem-solving Finn uses 3 metres of wood to build a ramp for wheelchair access to a door.
He wants the vertical height of the ramp to be 0.3 m.
What angle does the wood need to make with the ground?

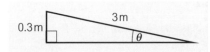

4 Real / Problem-solving A ship sails 130 km north and 180 km east.
On what bearing has it travelled?

Write the bearing using three figures.

Check Tick each box as your **confidence** in this topic improves.

Need extra help? Go to pages 110 and 111 and tick the boxes next to Q6–12. Then try them once you've finished 11.1–11.5.

1 Choose the trigonometric ratio and work out x.

a 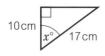 10cm, 17cm, $x°$

b 7cm, $x°$, 15cm

c 13cm, 18cm, $x°$

 2 **Real / Problem-solving** A plane flies for 200 km on a bearing of 050°.

  a How far east has the plane travelled?

  b How far north has it travelled?

 3 **Problem-solving** Work out the area of this isosceles triangle.

You need to find the height of the triangle first.

 4 **Problem-solving** Calculate the size of angle θ in this diagram.

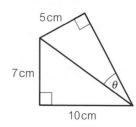

 5 **Problem-solving** Work out the angle between AD and AC.

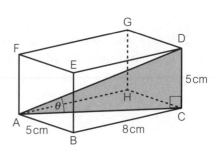

Check Tick each box as your **confidence** in this topic improves. ☹ 😐 ☺ ▢ ▢ ▢

Need extra help? Go to page 111 and tick the boxes next to Q13–15. Then try them once you've finished 11.1–11.5.

Unknown sides

1 Label each triangle with

    i 'opp' on the side opposite to angle θ

    ii 'adj' on the adjacent side

    iii 'hyp' on the hypotenuse.

a
b
c

2 For each triangle

    i write the tangent ratio

    ii write the sine ratio

    iii write the cosine ratio.

The three trigonometric ratios can be remembered using the phrase

    SOH   **CAH**   **TOA**

    $\dfrac{\text{Opp}}{\text{Sin}\,\theta \times \text{Hyp}}$ $\dfrac{\text{Adj}}{\text{Cos}\,\theta \times \text{Hyp}}$ $\dfrac{\text{Opp}}{\text{Tan}\,\theta \times \text{Hyp}}$

a
b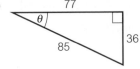
c

3 Work out x, correct to 1 d. p.

a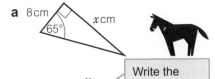
b
c

tan ...... $= \dfrac{x}{\square}$ [Write the tangent ratio.]

$x = $ ...... $\times$ tan ......   [Rearrange.]

$x = $ ....   [Use a calculator to work out x.]

sin ...... $= \dfrac{x}{\square}$

$x = $ ...... $\times$ sin ......

$x = $ ....

cos ...... $= \dfrac{x}{\square}$

4 Follow these steps to work out the value of x.

    a On the triangle, label the sides that you have been given or need to find.

    b Choose the trigonometric ratio you are going to use.

    c Write the ratio.

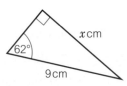

    d Rearrange to find x.

Strategy hint

Label the sides of the triangle opp, adj and hyp.
Which ones are you using?

    e Use your calculator to work out the missing side.

5 Work out the length of each side marked with a letter.

Follow the same method as in Q4.

a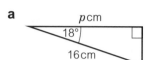
p cm
18°
16 cm

b
9 cm
q cm
42°

c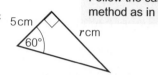
5 cm
60°
r cm

Unknown angles

6 Use the $\sin^{-1}$ function on your calculator to work out θ.

a $\sin \theta = \frac{7}{10}$ **b** $\sin \theta = 0.25$

Rearrange to make θ the subject. The inverse of sin is $\sin^{-1}$.
$\theta = \sin^{-1}\frac{7}{10}$

SHIFT sin ($\frac{7}{10}$) =

7 Use the $\cos^{-1}$ function on your calculator to work out θ.

a $\cos \theta = \frac{5}{8}$ **b** $\cos \theta = 0.8$

8 Use the $\tan^{-1}$ function on your calculator to work out θ.

a $\tan \theta = \frac{3}{10}$ **b** $\tan \theta = 0.7$

9 Work out the missing angle, correct to 1 d.p.

a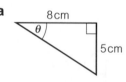
8 cm
θ
5 cm

b
θ
15 cm
9 cm

c
12 cm
θ
7 cm

Guided

$\tan \theta = \frac{\square}{\square}$ ⟵ Write the tangent ratio.

$\theta = \tan^{-1} \frac{\square}{\square}$ ⟵ Rearrange.

$\theta = \ldots\ldots\ldots$ ⟵ Use a calculator to work out θ.

$\sin \theta = \frac{\square}{\square}$

$\theta = \sin^{-1} \frac{\square}{\square}$

$\theta = \ldots\ldots\ldots$

$\cos \theta = \frac{\square}{\square}$

$\theta = \cos^{-1} \frac{\square}{\square}$

$\theta = \ldots\ldots\ldots$

10 Follow these steps to work out the size of angle θ.

a On the triangle, label the sides that you have been given or need to find.

b Choose the trigonometric ratio you are going to use.

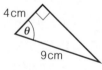
4 cm
θ
9 cm

c Write the ratio.

d Rearrange to make θ the subject.

e Use your calculator to work out the missing angle.

11 Work out the missing angle in each triangle.
You need to decide which ratio to use.

Follow the same method as in Q10.

a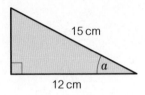

b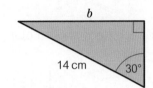

c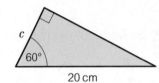

12 Work out the missing angle or side in each triangle.
You need to decide which ratio to use.

a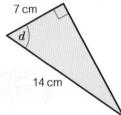

b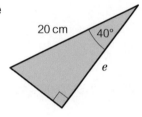

c

d 7 cm

e

Solving problems

13 Real / Modelling Jamie wants to find the height his ladder
reaches when up against the house. The ladder is 6 m long.
The angle between the ladder and the ground is 72°.

Draw a sketch of the
right-angled triangle.
What information
have you already
been given?

a Work out which trigonometric ratio Jamie needs to use.

b Calculate the height the ladder reaches up the house.

14 Real / Problem-solving A ship sails 50 km east and then 70 km north.
What is the bearing of the ship from its original position?

15 Problem-solving Work out the height of this isosceles triangle.

Split the triangle in half to make a
right-angled triangle.

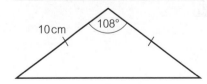

1 Work out the lengths of the sides marked with letters.

a

b

c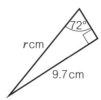

2 Work out the missing angle for each right-angled triangle.

a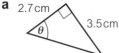

b

c

3 Modelling / Problem-solving A ship leaves port and travels on a bearing of 255° for 53.8 km.

Strategy hint

Sketch a diagram to help.

a How far west has it travelled?

b How far south has it travelled?

4 Problem-solving In this triangle XZ is perpendicular to WY.

a Calculate the size angle XYZ.

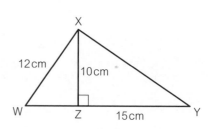

b Calculate the size angle XWZ.

c Using your answers to part **a** and **b**, calculate the size of angle WXY.

5 Problem-solving Work out the size of angle θ.

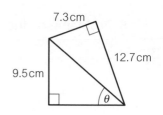

6 In this room, a motion sensor for a burglar alarm system is mounted at the midpoint of PQ.

a Work out the horizontal distance from R to the motion sensor.

The motion sensor is 2.1 m off the ground.

b Work out the angle between R and the motion sensor.

P ——————— S

3.8 m

Q ———— 5 m ———— R

7 The diagram shows a cuboid.
Calculate

a the length AG

$AG = \sqrt{4^2 + 8^2} = $ ....

b the angle between AG and AF

AHG is a right-angled triangle.
Use Pythagoras' theorem.
$AH^2 + GH^2 = AG^2$
$AG = \square$

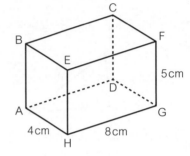

c the length of the diagonal AF.

8 The diagram shows a square-based pyramid.
The vertex T of the pyramid is over the centre
of the square base and is 12 cm above the base.
Calculate

a the length PR

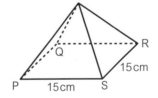

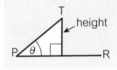

b the size of angle TPR

Worked example

c the length PT.

9 A family is walking towards the Great Pyramid of Giza. The pyramid is 139 m tall and the family
observe that the top is at an angle of 20° to the horizontal. After they have walked 4 minutes
nearer, it is observed that the top of the pyramid is now at an angle of 80° to the horizontal.

a How far have the family walked?

b At what speed was the family walking? Give your answer in m/s.

1 Write these ratios as fractions for this right-angled triangle.

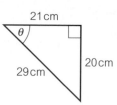

a sin θ .... **b** cos θ .... **c** tan θ ....

2 Work out the value of x. You need to decide which function to use.

a

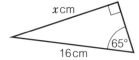

b

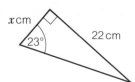

3 Find the missing angle for each triangle.

a

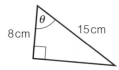

b

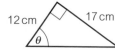

4 A ramp of 4 m makes an angle of 20° with the ground.
How high is the ramp above the ground?

5 **a** Work out the height of this isosceles triangle.

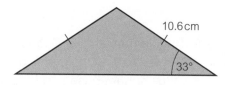

b Work out the length of the base.

c Work out the area of the triangle.

6 The diagram shows a circle with centre O and radius 8 cm.
Find the length of the chord AB.

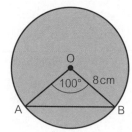

7 The diagram shows a cube with side lengths 12 cm.
Calculate

a the length AG
b the angle between AG and AF

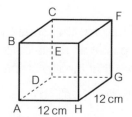

c the length of the diagonal AF.

1 Set P contains the first five prime numbers.

a Write set P using set notation.

b Is 1 ∈ P? Explain your answer.

c Is {even number} 2 P. Explain your answer.

> Curly brackets { } are used to show a set of values.
> ∈ means 'is an element of' or a member of a set. Elements are usually numbers, but could also be letters, subjects or even animals.
> ∉ means is not an element of a set.

2 Reasoning A = {2, 4, 6, 7, 10} and B = {square numbers}.
C is the set of elements that are in both A and B.
Write set C using set notation.

3 A is the set of the first 5 multiples of 4.
B is the set of the first 5 square numbers.
Use set notation to list the elements of

a A

b B

c A ∩ B

d Complete the Venn diagram.

Now list the elements of

e A'

f B'

g A ∪ B

> ξ means the universal set.
> A Venn diagram shows sets of data in circles inside a rectangle. You write data that is in both sets in the part where the circles overlap.
> A ∩ B represents the elements that are in both A and B.
> A ∪ B represents the elements that are A or B or both.
> A' represents the elements not in A.

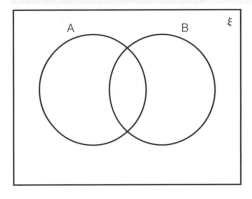

4 ξ = {1, 2, 3, ... 15}
A = {Even numbers}
B = {Multiples of 3}

a Complete the Venn diagram.

b List the elements of these sets.

i A ∪ B

ii A ∩ B

iii A'

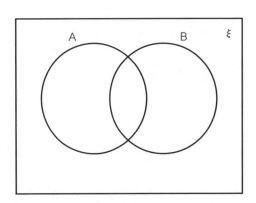

Check   Tick each box as your **confidence** in this topic improves.   ☹ 😐 ☺   **Need extra help?** Go to page 119 and tick the box next to Q1. Then try it once you've finished 12.1–12.4.

Guided

1 Jaswinder rolls a 4-sided dice and flips a coin.

   a Write all the possible outcomes in the sample space diagram.

   b How many outcomes are there altogether? ....

   c Work out

   i P(even number and a head) ....

   ii P(1) ....   With head or tail.

   iii P(a number greater than 1 and a tail). ....

	H	T
1	H, 1	
2		T, 2
3		
4		

A sample space diagram shows all
the possible outcomes of two events.

2 In a probability experiment, Sachiko spun this fair spinner twice
and added the results together.

   a Complete the sample space diagram.

   b How many possible outcomes are there? ....

Guided

   c Which total is most likely? ....

   d Work out the probability that the total is

   i 2 ....

   ii 5 ....

   iii greater than 4. ....

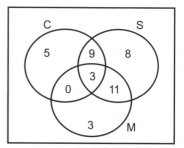

		First spin			
		1	2	3	4
Second spin	1	2			
	2				
	3				
	4				

3 The Venn diagram shows students' snacks of crisps (C),
sandwiches (S) or muesli bars (M).

   a How many students had crisps, sandwiches and a muesli bar?

   b How many students had crisps and sandwiches but not a
   muesli bar?

   c What is the probability that one of these students, picked at random,
   had a muesli bar?

How many students were
asked altogether?

4 Finn always hits 3, 19 or 7 with a dart.
He throws two darts and adds their scores.

   a Draw a sample space diagram to show his possible outcomes.

   b What is the probability that his total score will be

   i 38 ....

   ii less than 20 ....

   iii at least 20? ....

Check Tick each box as your
confidence in this
topic improves.

Need extra help? Go to pages 119 and 120
and tick the boxes next to Q2 and 3. Then try
them once you've finished 12.1–12.4.

116

Guided

1 There are 5 red counters and 3 blue counters in a bag. Elliyah picks a counter at random and then replaces it. Then she picks another one.

> A tree diagram shows two or more events and their probabilities.

a Complete the tree diagram to show the probabilities.

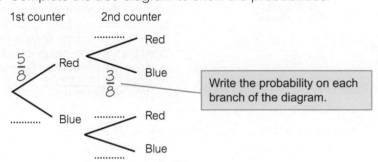

1st counter   2nd counter

$\frac{5}{8}$ Red

.... Red

.... Blue

$\frac{3}{8}$ Blue

> Write the probability on each branch of the diagram.

.... Blue   .... Red

.... Blue

> Two events are independent if one happening does not affect the probability of the other. For example, flipping heads with a coin has no effect on rolling an even number with a dice, so they are independent events.

b What is the probability of picking two red counters? ....

$\frac{5}{8} \times \frac{5}{8} = ...$

> Go along the branches for Red, Red. The 1st and 2nd counters are independent, so multiply the probabilities.

c What is the probability of one red and one blue counter?

$\frac{5}{8} \times \frac{3}{8} = ...$

> Go along the branches for Red, Blue.

$\frac{3}{8} \times \frac{5}{8} = ...$

> Go along the branches for Blue, Red.

.... + ... = ...

> Add their probabilities.

> To find the probability of two independent events one after the other, multiply their probabilities.
> P(A and B) = P(A) × P(B)

2 These letters are placed in a bag.

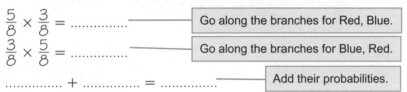

| A | C | F | O | P | T |

> If one event depends upon the outcome of another event, the two events are dependent events. For example, removing a red card from a pack of playing cards reduces the chance of choosing another red card. A tree diagram can be used to solve problems involving dependent events.

a Nasima removes a vowel from the bag and doesn't replace it. What was the probability of picking a vowel? ....

b How many letters are left in the bag? ....

c Yinka picks a letter from the bag. What is the probability of getting a vowel this time? ....

d Complete the tree diagram.

e What is the probability that

   i both vowels are picked

   ii first a vowel and then a consonant is picked

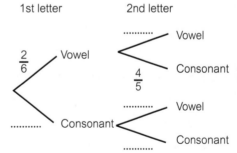

1st letter   2nd letter

$\frac{2}{6}$ Vowel

.... Vowel

$\frac{4}{5}$ Consonant

.... Consonant

.... Vowel

.... Consonant

> **Worked example**
>
>

   iii exactly one consonant is picked?

Check   Tick each box as your **confidence** in this topic improves.   ☹ 😐 ☺   **Need extra help?** Go to page 120 and tick the boxes next to Q4 and 5. Then try them once you've finished 12.1–12.4.

117

1 Sally dropped a drawing pin on the table lots of times. It landed either point up or point down. She recorded the results in a frequency table.

Position	Frequency
Point up	37
Point down	13

> In a probability experiment a trial is repeated many times and the outcomes recorded. For example, flipping a coin 100 times and recording heads or tails. The relative frequency of an outcome is called the experimental probability.
> Experimental probability of an outcome $= \dfrac{\text{frequency of outcome}}{\text{total number of trials}}$

a Work out the total frequency. ....

b Work out the experimental probability of the pin landing

   i point up ....   **ii** point down. ....

c She drops the pin 100 times. How many times do you expect it to land point up?

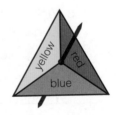

Guided

2 From a normal pack of cards, what is the theoretical probability of picking

   a a Queen $P(Queen) = \dfrac{\cdots}{52}$ There are ☐ Queens in a pack of cards.

   b a Club? ....

      Altogether, there are 52 cards in a pack.

> Theoretical probability is calculated without doing an experiment. For example, the theoretical probability of rolling a 4 with an ordinary dice is $\frac{1}{6}$.

3 a An ordinary 6-sided dice is rolled 150 times.
    How many times do you expect a 2?

> Theoretical probability can be used to calculate the frequencies you would expect in an experiment.

   b An ordinary pack of playing cards is shuffled and the top card turned over 100 times.
     How many times do you expect the top card to be a Heart?

   c A bag contains 3 red marbles and 7 blue marbles.
     A marble is picked at random and then replaced, 80 times.
     How many blue marbles do you expect to be picked?

4 Reasoning In a game, players use this spinner to move around the board.

   a What is the theoretical probability of landing on red if the spinner is fair?

   b How many times would you expect the spinner to land on each colour in 150 spins?

The table shows the results for 150 spins.

   c Theia says that the spinner is fair.
     Do you agree? ....
     What could she do to be more confident that the spinner is fair?

Colour	Red	Blue	Yellow
Frequency	47	54	49

Check   Tick each box as your **confidence** in this topic improves.   **Need extra help?** Go to page 120 and tick the box next to Q6. Then try it once you've finished 12.1–12.4.

118

Set notation and Venn diagrams

1 **Problem-solving / Reasoning** 80 students are asked which sports clubs they belong to.
The results are:
hockey (H) 34, swimming (S) 38 and volleyball (V) 42.

 a Complete the Venn diagram.

 b How many students are not members of a sports club? ....

Probability diagrams

2 Agniv rolls the fair 6-sided dice and spins the spinner.

 a Draw a sample space diagram to show all the possible outcomes. How many are there?

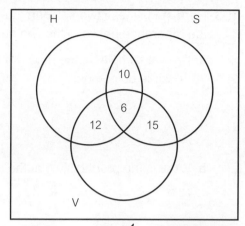

Put the dice scores across and the spinner scores down.

Worked example

 b Work out the probability of

 i a 5 on the dice ....

 ii one number being half of the other

 iii both numbers being at least 2.

 c Which is more likely: two even numbers or two odd numbers? ....

 Agniv rolls the dice and spins the spinner and then adds the two numbers together.

 d Draw a new sample space diagram to show the total scores.

 e Which total score is the most likely?

 f What is the probability of scoring a total of at least 4?

3 Haru spins these two spinners and finds the difference between the two numbers.

a Draw a sample space diagram to show the possible outcomes.

b What is the probability that the outcome will be

i 5 **ii** 2 **iii** more than 3?

Tree diagrams

4 The tree diagram shows the probabilities of picking red marbles and blue marbles from a bag.

a Work out the probability of picking two reds.

1st pick 2nd pick

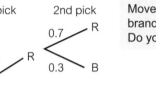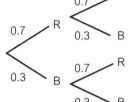

> Move your finger along the branches for Red, Red. Do you add or multiply?

b Work out the probability of picking

i red then blue (R, B)

ii blue then red (B, R)

> This means (R, B) or (B, R). Is the probability of these two outcomes greater than the probability of just one of them? Do you add or multiply?

iii red and blue in either order.

5 Jia kicks two penalties. The probability that she scores a goal is 0.7 for each kick.

a Draw a tree diagram to show the outcomes and their probabilities.

b Work out the probability that she gets exactly one goal.

Experimental and theoretical probability

6 A doctors' surgery records information about the first 50 people to arrive for treatment.
Some of the information is shown in the table.

	Male	Female	Total
Adult	11		26
Child		4	
Total			50

a Complete the table.

11 + ☐ = 26

b Find the probability that the next person to arrive for treatment is an adult female.

1 A = {1, 2, 3, 4, 5, 6, 7, 8}

 B = {2, 4, 6, 8, 10}

 C = {3, 6, 9}

 a How many elements are in set A?

 b Erina has written '9 ∉ B'. is she correct? Explain your answer.

 c Vijay has written 'C ∈ A'. is he correct? Explain your answer.

2 The Venn diagram shows people's choices of vanilla (V), strawberry (S) or chocolate (C) flavour ice cream in a restaurant.

 a How many people had

   i three different flavours ....

   ii only one flavour? ....

 b How many people chose ice cream as a dessert?

   ....

 c What is the probability that one of these people, picked at random, had two different flavours?

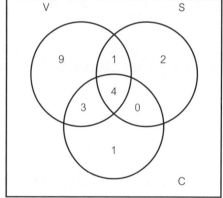

3 Akram and Hassan play badminton together.
 Based on previous games, Akram is three times as likely to win as Hassan.
 Work out the probability that Akram will win only one of the next two games.

 > Work out the probability that Akram will win a game.
 > Draw a tree diagram.

4 Draw a tree diagram to show the probabilities of picking a milk (M), a dark (D) or a white (W) chocolate at random from this box, eating it, and then picking another chocolate at random.

First chocolate   Second chocolate

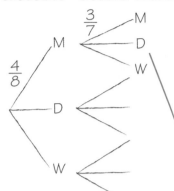

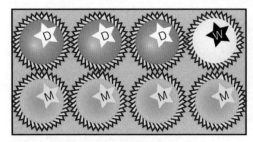

Worked example

If you've already eaten a milk chocolate, there are only 3 milk chocolates left. There are 7 chocolates left in total.

Work out the probability of picking

a two dark chocolates

b at least one milk chocolate.

5 Reasoning Jabir placed some red and yellow marbles in a bag. He drew this tree diagram to show the probabilities of taking two marbles from the bag at random, one at a time.

a Was the first marble replaced in the bag before the second marble was taken? Explain your answer.

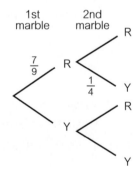

1st marble   2nd marble

b Complete the tree diagram.

c Work out the probability of taking two different coloured marbles.

6 Reasoning A drawer contains 20 socks that are black, brown or blue. The probability that two socks chosen at random are both brown is $\frac{1}{9}$. How many brown socks are in the drawer? Explain your answer.

1 A = {1, 2, 3, 4, 5, 6, 7, 8}

B = {2, 4, 6, 8, 10}

C = {3, 6, 9}

Represent this information in the Venn diagram.

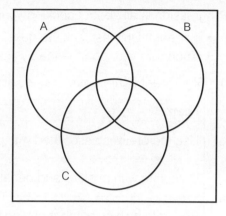

2 **Problem-solving** A quiz team consists of five members. Three are female and two are male. In a certain quiz, three team members are chosen at random to answer questions. What is the probability that two males and one female are chosen?

3 A fair 4-sided spinner and a fair 6-sided spinner are numbered 1–4 and 1–6, respectively. Both spinners are spun and their scores are added. What is the most likely total?

4 **Real / Modelling** Fayaz is learning to ride a skateboard. He predicts that the chance of doing a stunt called a fakie is 0.6 on his first attempt and 0.7 on his second attempt.

a Complete the tree diagram to show the possible outcomes of his first two attempts.

b Work out the probability that Fayaz succeeds with both of his attempts at a fakie.

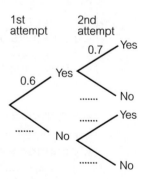

Progression charts

Progression is all about checking your confidence in the maths that you're learning.

- For each Unit test, tick the questions you answered correctly.
- Then rate your confidence by ticking a smiley face.

1 Significant figures, powers and standard form

I can...	Unit 1: Unit test			
Use the prefixes associated with powers of 10.	Q1 ☐			
Calculate with positive and negative powers.	Q3 ☐			
Round to a given number of significant figures.	Q2 ☐			
Write numbers using standard form.	Q4 ☐			
Calculate with numbers written in standard form.	Q5 ☐	Q6 ☐	Q7 ☐	Q8 ☐
My confidence ☹○ ☺○ ☺○				

2 2D shapes and 3D solids

I can...	Unit 2: Unit test	
Calculate the surface area and volume of prisms and cylinders.	Q3 ☐	Q5 ☐
Calculate the circumference and area of circles and sectors.	Q1 ☐	
Use Pythagoras' theorem in right-angled triangles.	Q2 ☐	Q4 ☐
My confidence ☹○ ☺○ ☺○		

3 Quadratics

I can...	Unit 3: Unit test		
Find the general term of an arithmetic sequence.	Q1 ☐		
Recognise and continue geometric sequences.	Q4 ☐		
Expand pairs of linear expressions.	Q2 ☐	Q3 ☐	Q5 ☐
Factorise quadratic expressions into two brackets.	Q6 ☐	Q7 ☐	
Solve quadratic equations by factorising.	Q8 ☐		
My confidence ☹○ ☺○ ☺○			

4 Constructions

I can...	Unit 4: Unit test			
Bisect lines using a ruler and compasses.	Q2 ☐		Q3 ☐	
Bisect angles using a ruler and compasses.	Q1 ☐		Q2 ☐	
Construct nets of 3D solids using a ruler and compasses.	Q4 ☐			
My confidence ☹○ ☺○ ☺○				

5 Inequalities, equations and formulae

I can...	Unit 5: Unit test		
Substitute values into expressions involving powers, roots and brackets.	Q1 ☐		
Solve linear inequalities and represent the solution on a number line.	Q4 ☐		
Use index laws with zero and negative powers.	Q2 ☐	Q3 ☐	
Expand and factorise expressions involving powers.	Q6 ☐	Q7 ☐	
Construct and solve complex equations.	Q5 ☐		
Change the subject of a formula.	Q8 ☐		
My confidence ☹○ ☺○ ☺○			

6 Collecting and analysing data

I can...	Unit 6: Unit test		
Choose a suitable sample size.	Q1 ☐	Q2 ☐	
Understand how to reduce bias in sampling and questionnaires.	Q3 ☐		
Design and use data collection sheets and tables.	Q4 ☐		
Construct and use a line of best fit to estimate missing values.	Q5 ☐		
Identify and explain outliers.	Q5b ☐		
Estimate the mean from a grouped frequency table.	Q6 ☐		
My confidence ☹○ ☺○ ☺○			

7 Multiplicative reasoning

I can...	Unit 7: Unit test
Recognise data sets that are in proportion and set up equations that show direct proportion.	Q1 ☐ Q2 ☐ Q5 ☐
Enlarge shapes using positive, negative and fractional scale factors, about a centre of enlargement.	Q3 ☐
Describe an enlargement on a coordinate grid.	Q3b ☐
Understand and use column vectors in translations.	Q4 ☐
Find an original value using inverse operations.	Q6 ☐
Calculate percentage change.	Q7 ☐
My confidence ☹◯ 😐◯ ☺◯	

8 Scale drawings and measures

I can...	Unit 8: Unit test
Use scales in maps and plans.	Q1 ☐ Q2 ☐
Use and measure bearings and solve angle problems involving bearings.	Q3 ☐
Know and use the criteria for congruence of triangles and begin to use congruency to solve simple problems in triangles.	Q4 ☐
Use similarity to solve problems in 2D shapes.	Q5 ☐
My confidence ☹◯ 😐◯ ☺◯	

9 Accuracy and measures

I can...	Unit 9: Unit test
Solve problems involving rates of change.	Q3 ☐
Convert units with compound measures.	Q4 ☐
Calculate density and pressure.	Q5 ☐ Q6 ☐
Find upper and lower bounds.	Q1 ☐ Q2 ☐ Q7 ☐
My confidence ☹◯ 😐◯ ☺◯	

10 Graphical solutions

I can...	Unit 10: Unit test
Draw graphs with equation $ax + by = c$.	Q5 ☐
Recognise that equations of the form $y = mx + c$ are straight-line graphs, and state their gradient (m) and intercept (0, c).	Q2 ☐
Understand and draw graphs of quadratic functions.	Q1 ☐
Solve a pair of simultaneous equations.	Q4 ☐
Solve a pair of linear simultaneous equations by drawing graphs.	Q5b ☐
Find the equation of the line between two points.	Q3 ☐
Solve more complex simultaneous equations.	Q6 ☐
My confidence ☹○ ☺○ ☺○	

11 Trigonometry

I can...	Unit 11: Unit test
Work out the sine, cosine and tangent of any angle.	Q1 ☐
Use the sine, cosine and tangent ratios to work out an unknown side in a right-angled triangle.	Q2 ☐
Use the trigonometric ratios to work out an unknown angle in a right-angled triangle.	Q3 ☐
Use trigonometry to solve problems involving missing lengths and angles.	Q4 ☐ Q5 ☐ Q6 ☐ Q7 ☐
My confidence ☹○ ☺○ ☺○	

12 Probability

I can...	Unit 12: Unit test
Use correct set language and notation. Present the possible outcomes of events using Venn diagrams.	Q1 ☐
Present the possible outcomes of two successive events using sample space diagrams.	Q3 ☐
Use tree diagrams to find probabilities of two or more events.	Q2 ☐ Q4 ☐
My confidence ☹○ ☺○ ☺○